Connections

A Journey to
Understanding

Frank Chodl

Psychic Medium

BALBOA.
PRESS
A DIVISION OF HAY HOUSE

Balboa Press books may be ordered through booksellers or by contacting:

Balboa Press
A Division of Hay House
1663 Liberty Drive
Bloomington, IN 47403
www.balboapress.com
1 (877) 407-4847

Because of the dynamic nature of the Internet, any web addresses or links contained in this book may have changed since publication and may no longer be valid. The views expressed in this work are solely those of the author and do not necessarily reflect the views of the publisher, and the publisher hereby disclaims any responsibility for them.

The author of this book does not dispense medical advice or prescribe the use of any technique as a form of treatment for physical, emotional, or medical problems without the advice of a physician, either directly or indirectly. The intent of the author is only to offer information of a general nature to help you in your quest for emotional and spiritual well-being. In the event you use any of the information in this book for yourself, which is your constitutional right, the author and the publisher assume no responsibility for your actions.

Any people depicted in stock imagery provided by Thinkstock are models, and such images are being used for illustrative purposes only. Certain stock imagery © Thinkstock.

Print information available on the last page.

ISBN: 978-1-5043-5303-8 (sc)
ISBN: 978-1-5043-5305-2 (hc)
ISBN: 978-1-5043-5304-5 (e)

Library of Congress Control Number: 2016903832

Balboa Press rev. date: 04/22/2016

Contents

Special Thanks

To my Editor and dear friend, LauraKatherine Logan, for her meticulous attention to detail, and to all of those who contributed their experiences to this book.

Dedication

To my wife and partner, Betz McKeown, without whose support, encouragement, and love this book would still be a work in progress.

Introduction

This life has been an exciting adventure of lessons learned through each and every psychic and metaphysical encounter. This book is written for people who have experienced phenomena that they have trouble explaining to those who haven't. It is NOT intended to turn anyone into a psychic or a medium. Rather, it's my intention to give you a fuller understanding of what you experience; give you a way to define your experiences in order to better explain them to others; and open you up to more, deeper, clearer, and safer experiences. It is my hope that you, dear reader, will look at my experiences and what I have learned from them and find a path that leads you to the answers you are seeking.

The accounts related in this book are true and depicted as accurately as possible. In cases where the client wished to keep their identity confidential or where the client was unavailable, I refer to them by an initial only rather than by name.

Chapter 1

Psychic or Medium?

Who Am I?

Let me start by saying that I am a psychic, a medium, a healer, a teacher, and above all, a student.

A psychic is a seer. They can see events that have happened in the past (clairvoyant), see things as they are happening while not physically being at the same place (telepathic), and/or see things that will happen in the future (precognitive). Extra Sensory Perception (ESP) is often passed off as a lucky guess or an intuitive assumption. But, how do we explain the extremely accurate relating of specific facts and minute details when the information about the person, event, or object is or has not been made available?

A medium is a go-between, the conduit for interaction between persons living on this physical plane of existence and those who have died. Many mediums like myself depend on the aid of entities who are fully aware of both sides of the veil. They are often referred to as guides or Guardian Angels. Yes, I speak to dead people. Or, more accurately, they speak to me and, with the help of my Guide, Marie, I translate for them.

I was first identified as a psychic medium in 1975 by Ed and Lorraine Warren, founders of the New England Society for Psychic Research in Monroe, CT (www.warrens.net). At that time, I didn't realize the differences between psychics, mediums, and psychic mediums. John Edward, (http://johnedward.net/#), defines it this way: "Psychics perceive, mediums receive." I explain it this way: A psychic will walk into a house he has never been in before and tell you where your missing keys are. A medium will walk into the house and tell you who moved them and why. A psychic medium will do both.

A healer helps to make others whole, whether in body, mind, or spirit. A medium can be a healer in that he/she helps to bring awareness and understanding to those involved on both sides, which facilitates their own healing from within. Healing may also come in the form of closure, resolution, acceptance, or departure. Very often what we need for healing is not necessarily what we wanted or expected. How often can we truly say that our wants, expectations, and true needs are in total alignment? Our guides are not bound by the three dimensional confines of this world. They can see past our wants and expectations and thus attend to our true needs.

A teacher shares his acquired knowledge and skills with others in order to help them realize their own understanding. A student realizes that, no matter how much he thinks he has learned, there is infinitely more to learn.

This book chronicles my journey thus far with the learning and understanding that I have acquired along the way. For me personally, it also brings so many of my experiences and lessons together. In doing this, it gives me a clearer vision of the work ahead of me, of which I am called to do. I am a medium, a connector, a healer, the conduit for interaction between persons living on this plane of existence and for those who have died. I speak to dead people and they speak to and through me. I carry the messages of healing for both sides of the veil.

Meeting My Guide

It was in the autumn of 1964. I was eight years old. My younger sister and I were playing in my bedroom of the small apartment we lived in, upstairs from my maternal grandparents.

The house in Auburn, NY where I first met my guide.

It must have been early in the evening because the room was dim, though no lights were on yet. While we were playing with our toys on the floor, I suddenly saw a woman appear to my left as if she had just come through the door from my sisters' room. The door was closed and I had not heard the familiar squeak of the old hinges. Yet, there she was. I would estimate that she was in her late 20s or early 30s. She had long dark hair that fell straight down over her shoulders and back. She wore a long bed gown or simple dress that covered her from neck to toe. All of this detail I could clearly see, yet she was entirely pale blue in color and almost transparent.

The woman moved effortlessly, as if floating across the room to the closet door to my right. The whole apparition lasted less than ten seconds, then she passed right through the closed door and she was gone. Even at my young age, I silently questioned whether I had actually seen what I thought I had or if it was my imagination playing games with me. That was, until my sister asked me if I had just seen the woman.

This had been my first conscious psychic experience. Many times after that, I would hear or see objects move and doors open and close in that old house when there was no one near and no other logical explanation such as the wind coming through a window or gravity pulling at something that was perched precariously. Soon I began to realize that I could feel the presence of the woman whenever these events occurred. I could feel her cold yet comforting embrace envelop me as if she was hugging me to protect me from any danger. I felt calm and safe whenever she came to me.

During one of my college art classes I had been given an assignment to "paint something." There is nothing more intimidating on the face of this planet than a blank canvas. As I stared at the white space my hand began to reach for tubes of paint. There was no conscious thought about which colors I was applying to the pallet. Then, just as if someone had gently taken my hand, I began to paint. This was not unlike automatic writing except that I wasn't in a trance. I was clearly conscious of everything that was happening.

Brushstroke after brushstroke, one color after another, my hand was moving faster than I had ever painted before. My hand was frenetically moving all around the canvas as the picture revealed itself. Within only a few hours the painting was complete. It depicted a woman in her late 20s or early 30s. She had long dark hair that fell straight down over her shoulders and back. She wore a long bed gown or simple dress that covered her from neck to toe. She was no longer entirely pale blue in color and almost transparent. She now had substance. You can see a face. Her hand is beckoning you to follow her through a doorway that floats in space and on down the hallway into the light. She is my guide. All I did was hold the brush while she revealed herself to me.

Whenever there is a need and I think about the vision of her, my guide comes to me in order to open a safe passage for contact with others from that plane. She wraps around me. I feel the cold and peaceful calm that is her. I shiver and tremble from the cold but it's not at all uncomfortable. Tears run down my cheeks and yet I am not the least bit sad. Many people have reported that they have felt the ice cold air emanating all around my body during these sessions, even in the most sweltering environments.

Marie's "self-portrait."

Inheritance

Every member of my family on my mother's side has a small scar on the right wrist. When I first saw the scar I asked my mother if I had ever been cut there. She showed me that she also had the scar and explained how my sisters, her mother, and her siblings all had it, too. We were all born with the mark. When my son was born the first thing I looked for was the mark, and there it was.

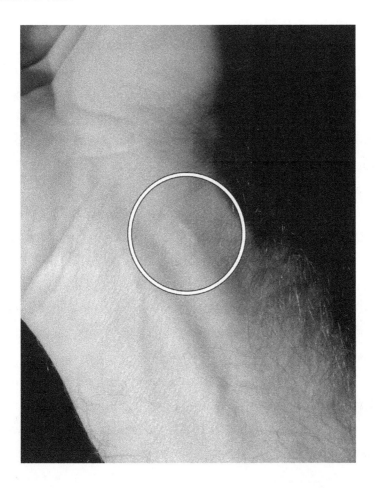

Recurring birthmarks have been linked to past life traumas. When the mark manifests throughout a family, the bond can manifest in many ways. The telepathic connections among all the members of my family are extremely strong.

When I was born, my family lived in St. Charles, Illinois, just west of Chicago. On two separate occasions, my mother announced to my father, almost to the minute, that her sister had experienced a miscarriage. Her sister lived in Rome, New York, over 700 miles away and my mother had not been informed that her sister was pregnant.

How many times, before the days of caller ID, have you heard a phone ring and knew who it was before you answered it? Is it purely intuition, coincidence, logical inference based on details surrounding the event, or just a lucky guess? The ability to relate specific details that were not revealed prior to or during the event takes perceiving those events out of the realm of a "lucky guess."

One day in 1970, when I was 14, my mother got a phone call. I remember watching her raise the receiver to her ear as if in slow motion. Before she could ask who was calling I fell back against the door frame and gasped, "Oh my God, he's had a stroke!" At that age I'm not sure I even knew what a stroke was. My mother turned to me with a puzzled look and proceeded to answer the call.

About halfway into the conversation her look turned from bewilderment to shock. It was an aunt telling mom that my grandfather, their father, had just suffered a stroke and was taken to the hospital. He never came home.

My Babci (Polish for grandmother and pronounced Bahb-she) ruled the roost. She was, without question, the head of the family. My Dzadzu (Polish for grandfather and pronounced Jah-jew) on the other hand, was the nurturer of the family and was dearly loved by everyone. On the day he died, almost to the minute, a shockwave reverberated throughout the family. My younger sister slashed the side of her hand with a razor blade while cutting a plastic mold off of a candle she was making. My older sister became violently ill at the college she was attending 100 miles away. Other events occurred simultaneously among all of my aunts' and uncles' families.

At the wake I stood at the back of the parlor and refused to go up to the coffin. Mom asked me why and I said to her, "That's not him up there. All my memories of him are alive and I don't want to remember him dead." Already, as a young teen, I knew that "he" was gone and all that was left in the casket was a shell.

Dzadzu (Karol Bochenek) and Babci (Katrzyna Niedzwiczski Bochenek) on their 50th wedding anniversary, 1967.

Family Ties

I entered college in the fall of 1973. One afternoon, while walking back to my dormitory from classes, I was overcome by a feeling that something was wrong at home. The more I walked the stronger the feeling became. It got clearer and clearer in my mind that the problem was within my family and had something to do with my younger sister. In what seemed like only a couple of minutes, I had walked several miles from campus and found myself at the edge of a river under a railroad trestle. (It took over an hour to walk back. This was the first time that I was aware of the time differences that occur during my psychic experiences.)

When I arrived back at my dorm room I immediately phoned home to ask my mother what the problem with my sister was. She confirmed my premonition without revealing any details and assured me that everything was going to be all right. Actually, I believe her exact words were, "Yes, there's a problem with your sister, but don't worry. I'll tell you all about it when you get home this weekend." If you really want to stress out a psychic tell him that his vision is correct but not to worry about it. That's like me telling you not to think about big white Alaskan polar bears for the next hour or two.

Well, my sister survived. She had gotten caught charging long distance phone calls to another number and had to make restitution. I learned that, while I need to pay attention to my feelings and the messages that come with them, I have to let them play out as they will. Getting stressed about something that you have no control over never solves the problem. You only end up with the same problems plus the stress.

Developing Psychic Abilities

I believe that all psychic abilities are innate to our spiritual being. An Olympic weightlifter can hoist 600 pounds over his head. I know that if I were to attempt that I would end up in the hospital or worse, even though we both possess exactly the same bones, muscles, tendons, ligaments and nervous system. The weightlifter has worked and exercised his muscles for years on end to develop his abilities. Over the years the muscles I would need to perform that task have atrophied and settled in to perform the tasks that are my routine.

I had an accident that fractured my right elbow. The joint was immobilized for several weeks as the bone began to knit. Afterward, it took weeks of physical therapy and months of exercise to regain the full use of the injured arm. In the same way, the skills and senses that we call paranormal or psychic reside in all of us, but, if not exercised, will also atrophy. They do not die away, however. They are still there, inside all of us. We need to start slowly (don't want to blow a hamstring), and gradually redevelop the skills we were endowed with so many lifetimes ago.

There are two things that are essential to realizing our innate abilities. First, you need to recognize your potential and accept the fact that you possess that potential. Too often we sell ourselves short. I don't know how many times I have heard students say, "I don't know the answer," or "I don't know how to do that," when in fact, they do know but are just afraid to accept their own capabilities. Again, it is the metacognitive recognition of what we know.

Consider the story of the elephant and the stick. When an elephant is very young, the trainers will chain its leg to a large post buried deep in the ground so that the baby elephant can't escape. As the elephant grows, the trainer reduces the size of the chain and the post to simply a piece of rope and a stick. The adult elephant could easily break free and run wild, but years of training have convinced the animal that this is not possible. Therefore, it no longer tries.

When we are children our psychic abilities are strong and unbridled. By the time we are in grade school, society has "taught" our abilities out of us in favor of the status quo.

During a Christmas break from college in 1974, I decided to take a job working at a small restaurant in the Finger Lakes region of New York. As if things weren't getting strange enough, a girlfriend offered to let me stay with her family in the upstairs casket storage room of their family's funeral home. It was close to the town where the restaurant was and her parents said I was welcome to stay for free. How could I refuse?

I had a small folding cot right in the middle of all of the coffins. Although I was awakened a few times by the creeks and groans of the old Victorian house, I never had any unusual experiences there. There really were no spirits haunting the place. After all, by the time the "clients" were brought there, they had already long passed.

That winter I amused myself by practicing some telekinesis. Making small objects move across the table or floor and chandeliers gently sway to music on the radio became fun and games, especially in a funeral home. I was never able to move large or heavy objects, although I am sure that with enough practice I could.

Second, in order to redevelop your psychic skills, you need to determine your purpose. This requires serious self-examination and introspection. When is the last time you sat down and were really honest with yourself? Confucius said that if you choose a job that you love you'll never work a day in your life. How many of us are willing to make the decision to give up what may be an even moderately stable lifestyle for the risk of the unknown by pursuing our heart's passion?

I love to play the drums. My "man cave" is filled with percussion instruments. Playing the drums makes me feel good. I know that if I truly invested my time and energy I could be a better drummer and maybe make some money at. Is it my passion, however? Not really. It's more of a distraction or hobby. My profession for the past 30 or so years has been my art and teaching. My true calling, however, is that of the medium and healer. It has taken me years to accept that fact and direct my life down this path. The more I accept myself, the stronger I become in my abilities.

Powerful Toys

There are a wide variety of tools that psychics use in order to help them clarify their readings. Numerology, tea leaves, I Ching coins, Fu Chu sticks, Runes, bones, gem stones, and magic scrying mirrors all provide a means to divine answers to our questions. I have had my "fortune" told by Tarot readers, palmists, and astrologers, and I have on occasion used a crystal ball or pendulum to focus my attention. While seemingly harmless, divination tools need to be used carefully and with a clear intention of the purpose to which they will be applied. They are not toys or games and can be dangerous when used carelessly.

College is a time when we allow ourselves to open up to new ideas and experiences. Unfortunately, not every encounter was pleasant or had a happy ending. Back at the fraternity house a few of the brothers had decided to have some fun and play with an Ouija Board. The board itself is a rather simple looking piece of decorated wood with the alphabet, numbers 0 through 9, yes, no, and Good Bye printed on it. Originally called a Spirit Board and dating back to as far as 500 BCE, the modern Ouija Board with its heart shaped "planchette," or pointer stylus, became popular as a divination tool in the 1890s and later as a Parker Brother's game in 1966. I came to find out, however, that this seemingly harmless toy could become something entirely different.

On this particular night, four of the brothers were gathered around the board in one of the upstairs bedrooms. It started out as a fun game of simple questions and the board appeared to be giving them the answers they expected. Slowly the answers shifted to falsehoods and then to threats. Suddenly it began to spell out their names and the names of family members. The boys had moved away from the board but the planchette was still moving, on its own. When I arrived and saw what was happening, I picked up the board and threw it across the room into an old, long unused fireplace. As the board hit the back wall of the chamber it burst into flames and crumbled to ash.

There could be any number of rational explanations for what had occurred. It could have been unconscious telekinesis that moved the planchette. Their excitement and enthusiasm may have created a collective energy field that "fed" the board. The laminated layers of the board may have acted like a capacitor to store the energy. Perhaps when I threw it, it struck the rough brick of the fire box and the friction caused a spark which ignited the board. Regardless, it made quite an impression on everyone in the room and I'm quite sure they never replaced the board.

Now, I have never claimed to be the brightest candle in the hallway and in college I did have a Ouija Board of my own. I did, however, keep the planchette locked in a trunk while the board was hung on a wall as decoration. One late afternoon my friend, Walter, and his girlfriend, B, came to visit me and my girlfriend in my dorm room. B began to stare at the board and within minutes she was transfixed. She started to speak to the board in a language we could not recognize. It had the rhythm and pacing of a language and there were pauses as if she was listening to the other side of a conversation.

Walt was not a small young man. He stood about 5' 9" and weighed about 235 pounds. B was 5' 4" and maybe 100 pounds. He tried to get her attention and then shake her out of her apparent trance. She picked him up like a toy and threw him across the room. At that point I pulled the board off of the wall and broke it over my knee into four quarters, forming a cross with the breaks. Suddenly, as if nothing had happened B was back with us. She refused to believe that anything had happened and was extremely angry with us for implying such a thing.

From that day on, B's personality shifted from a sweet, loving young girl to a vicious shrew who would use anything and anyone to get her way. She and Walt broke up soon after the event.

If we choose to utilize divination tools of any sort, it is critically important that we clearly declare our intentions for the highest good of all involved at the outset of any session. Leaving these tools open and unprotected makes them vulnerable to entities who we may not want to deal with. They are a focus, not only for us on this side, but also for those on the other.

Chapter 2

Awareness

What Is Religion?

I was raised Roman Catholic. Let me qualify that. I was raised Polish Roman Catholic. We like to joke that we are the masters when it comes to guilt. We will confess to anything, even if we haven't done it yet. I went to a Polish Catholic elementary school where the students were taught Polish grammar, reading, and writing along with English from kindergarten on up. In the second grade I began studying Latin so that I could be an altar boy. (1963 Vatican II changed the liturgy of the Holy Mass from Latin to English for the public.) By sixth grade I had been quite well-versed on the Bible and was a lead altar boy being readied for the seminary and eventual priesthood.

At about that time I began to question many of the "facts" of my beliefs. The Nuns who taught the classes were typically all in lock-step with the fundamental ideology. You either believe the literal word of the Bible (as they interpreted it) or you go to hell. The priests were a bit more academic but usually replied in vague, metaphoric terms that meant little or nothing to a 12-year-old. Meanwhile, the onset of puberty curtailed my plans for the seminary. All of a sudden that celibacy clause seemed like a little too much to ask.

As life would have it, my mother decided to buy a house and move to an area where I would enter a public high school. Out of the constant oversight of the church, I was able to begin my explorations of other religions and beliefs in earnest. The more that I searched for the differences in world religions, the more astonished I became. When you peel through the layers of dogma and ceremony, remove the names and titles of the deities, and disregard the hierarchical bureaucracy, all religions are fundamentally the same.

Religions typically identify an ultimate good or perfection and then establish means to attain acceptable levels of that good. This good is often personified as an entity, either natural or supernatural, in order to transform it from a conceptual to a physical state. Even customs that give the forces of nature deity status tend to anthropomorphize those forces. This was traditionally done in order to more easily explain these conceptual forces to primitive peoples whose entire frame of reference was physical. They were hunters, gatherers, farmers, fisherman, and laborers.

In geometry we accept that a point is a coordinate in space at the intersection of two or more lines. And a line is an infinite series of points. Go back 2000 years and try to explain these mathematical concepts to the people of that day. Likewise, try to explain the internet to your great-grandmother. Concepts are simplified in order to gain the acceptance (not necessarily understanding) of the masses. Fear and awe are often thrown into the mix in order to insure compliance.

Tribes formed around shared ideas and beliefs. From these beliefs the tribes derived rules and systems of behavior that benefited the tribe. Whenever the tribe encountered situations or phenomena they could not easily understand or control, they would attribute them to the forces. If those occurrences benefitted the tribe they were attributed to the gods. If they were deemed to have harmed the tribe they were the work of the evil forces.

The Bible identifies perfect good as God and his nemesis as Satan (Isaiah 14:12-15 and Ezekiel 28:12-19). The Book of Revelation foretells of a time when the forces of Satan will rise up in an apocalyptic battle with God, Jesus, and the Heavenly Host. Armageddon will destroy everything as we know it and result in a new order. Interestingly, in physics, when atoms become overly charged, either negative or positive, there can be a violent discharge, or flash, which we call static electricity. The larger the atomic imbalance, the bigger the bang. It is becoming more widely accepted that our universe, as we know it, began with a "Big Bang." It was this precise catastrophic event which set energy and matter in motion in order to allow for the development of all that we know today. Pope Francis, in his 2015 encyclical, embraced the idea that "The Big Bang, which is today posited as the origin of the world, does not contradict the divine act of creation; rather, it requires it."

What Is Life?

I have had clear memories of what I perceive to be many previous lifetimes. I lived in Asheville, NC in the early 1900s, was a native in the mountains of Tennessee, a nobleman in 16th century Madrid, and a close personal friend of Jesus. (By the way, as far as I can tell, I was not Jesus, nor Julius Cesar, nor Buddha.) How many times have you been in a situation where you just know the answer to a problem or know how to perform a specific task and you know that you've never studied or practiced that skill before? Do we divine the answers by linking into some cosmic hard drive or are we tapping into memories of experiences from lives past?

How can we explain reincarnation? I like to think of the human body as a vehicle. When you buy a new car you are so proud of it. You protect it, wash it, show it off to your friends, and take care of it when it needs service and repairs. As it ages its needs change, services become more frequent and involved. Finally, after some number of years, it has outlived its usefulness and you retire it in favor of a newer model. The old car is finally sent to deteriorate in a junk yard or recycled.

Through astral projection we can leave the "car" at home and "take a walk" wherever we want. Open the door and step out, if you will. When I connect with a spirit entity, I am also opening the door and inviting them in for a brief ride. When we die we shed the old vehicle. Just as you are not your car, you are not your body. We may shop around a bit but, in time, we may choose another body and life to inhabit. Even if the old body is kept "alive" through mechanical or chemical means, the spirit may have moved on. "Elvis has left the building."

What about those who have been kept alive for months or years in a vegetative state and then miraculously reawakened? During conscious astral projection a link is maintained between the spirit and the body. The spirit keeps the body alive in order to facilitate a safe return. Likewise, those in natural or artificial coma states, although not present, are still connected. If the need to continue the lessons in this lifetime is great enough and the vehicle is still viable, it is possible to get back behind the wheel and move on. If, however, the body physically dies, the connection is severed and the spirit can be set free to move on.

Sometimes people don't wait to change cars. For whatever reasons, they opt to end their own life. We can choose to trade it in at any time but there is often a penalty for early trade in.

At the end of each life level we cross over to a place of evaluation. Every level that we move through is like a grade that we enroll in. You have to master the challenges of third grade before you advance to fourth. Whether we pass, fail, or simply attend, each level gives us opportunities for the next. Our "free will" gives us the ability to decide how we are going to process what we have experienced. By the way, doing nothing at all and waiting for "nature to take its course" is also a decision we make of our own free will. If we have satisfactorily mastered the skills and tasks of that life we may move on to the next grade level. If not, we may have to return to work through any deficiencies. Those who traded in their vehicles early will have to try that level again.

We've all heard about or maybe even know someone who was declared dead or in an extended lifeless state like a coma and then miraculously came back to life. Often these people relate images of passing through a tunnel into light. (Coincidently, an interesting metaphor for birth).

Past Life Experiences

I moved from New York State to North Carolina in 1984 to follow the trend of the industrial migration from the north to south. As a commercial/industrial photographer I had to be where the business was. Something more than business attracted me to this area, however.

My first trip to Asheville was far more than a simple photo op. The city was alive with a psychic energy I hadn't felt since my college days. When I visited the Biltmore Estate (www. biltmore.com) I knew immediately that I was returning to a place I had never been to in this lifetime. I remembered the scenes in the displayed photographs that were over 100 years old as if they were just recent events. I knew the rooms and the passageways. I could describe what was in the next room before we got there. Although I was not a member of the family, I knew them all well and loved one of the daughters dearly. We would have wed had I been of their social stature. Somewhere in the stone wall surrounding the gardens is a stone with our initials scraped into it. Behind the stone is a memento of our love. Perhaps I will retrieve it someday.

My most recent ex-wife (material for another book) was very interested in the psychic phenomena that surround me. She had the desire to actively engage in the sessions but she hadn't developed the sensitivity to the energies that were involved. As a result, she tended to read a lot into situations that weren't really there.

It's easy for people to project their own feelings and desires into psychic communications. When the entity who you are receiving information from is neither visible nor audible, that disconnect can be very disturbing. To relieve the confusion, the mind tries to fill in the blanks with things that seem to make sense. "How could I possibly know about [that] if I wasn't the person who experienced it in a previous life?" This became very clear to me when she proclaimed that I was the reincarnation of Jesus and that she was Mary Magdalene. While I do believe that I knew him, I'm quite sure that I was not him. After that she insisted that she had been the woman at Biltmore Estate.

I never had the opportunity to meet my ex-wife's father as he had died several years before I met her. Often she had said that she felt him near. One evening so did I. He came through very clearly. He was deeply saddened because of something that had been unresolved. I was not told what the conflict was. That was between the two of them. The anguish that he was feeling, however, was profound. He cried out, "I am so sorry. So very sorry." My ex-wife never told me what that was all about but not long after that encounter she informed me that we could no longer be married. I guess I struck a nerve.

What Is Spirit?

Just as we have the will to decide if and how we are going to progress, we can decide whether we will use our knowledge for perfection or chaos. This is where the idea of balance comes into play. Sir Isaac Newton's (1642-1727) second law of physics states that "for every action there is an equal and opposite reaction." An example that he uses to explain this theory is that of a horse pulling a boulder. As the horse pulls on the rope, the tension on the rope pulls back on the horse. If we apply Newtonian physics to actions and deeds, it would stand to reason that for everything that is good there is something that is bad. Therefore, while we possess the will to choose our own actions, the repercussions of those actions are inverse, simultaneous, and inevitable. This theory works wonderfully for physical objects but falls short when it comes to the metaphysical.

John Calvin (1509-1564) proposed the idea that free will was a myth and that all actions, good or evil, were predetermined by God at the beginning of time and that God had already chosen those who would be saved and those who would be damned. If this were true, then nothing we do would be of any consequence in the overall scheme of existence. There would be no purpose to learning or spiritual growth.

Calvin's theory of predestination would tell us that if God had already decided that the rock would not be moved, nothing that the horse could do would move it. Consequently, there would be no equal or opposite reaction that would counter the predestined course of events.

Karmic law says that good actions reap good reactions and evil begets evil. The Bible echoes this when it says "As ye sow, so shall ye reap" (Galatians 6:7-9). However, Karma says that those reactions can happen anytime and/or anywhere in this or any subsequent lifetime. The universe will deliver its due.

Karma also recognizes the connection of everything living and non-living. The reactions to our actions are not limited to ourselves but affect everyone and everything around us. Likewise, the reactions of others to our actions affect everything around them, and so on and so on. It's a cosmic butterfly effect, if you will. The wind off the fluttering wings of a butterfly in Brazil disturbs the air which moves a leaf and leads to another reaction and ultimately causes a tsunami in Japan.

While exponentially mind boggling in its infinite series of outwardly expanding reactions to any single action, Karma is still inherently linear. Quantum physics takes this concept to an even more mind-wrenching level. Max Planck (1858-1947) would argue that there is no single universe or time. All time and space occur simultaneously and therefore interact and react simultaneously. Matter, at its most subatomic level does not act in the same way that we perceive the physical world. Energy, like the energy that constitutes our spiritual self, can move and reshape matter. Matter can even occupy two different places at the same time.

Biblical literalists claim that this is all impossible because God created everything in six days and that was that. I would argue that that idea limits the power of God to only finite creation. In his 2015 encyclical, Pope Francis states, "evolution of nature is not inconsistent with the notion of creation because evolution pre-supposes the creation of beings which evolve." When we consider the ability to create an organism that can evolve and adapt to changes in its environment and then expand that concept from a three dimensional planet to a multidimensional universe, thus imparting upon humanity the ability to evolve or grow on multiple levels, perhaps simultaneously, how much more awesome and powerful does our perception of God become?

Admittedly, my references to Karma, the Bible, Newtonian physics, and quantum physics are fairly basic. I encourage all readers to explore these and other theories. Every idea and concept conceived of man is limited to the scope of his or her knowledge. Likewise, our ability to explain and define our conceptions is biased by our own experiences and understanding. When any two persons try to recount a specific event, the truth of that event usually falls somewhere in the middle of the variations of their retellings because of their individualized interpretation of that event.

The Other Side

What is on the other side? Many religions and mythologies offer ideas of a place of ultimate grace and reward such as Heaven, Swarga, or Valhalla, but you usually have to qualify to get in. Are there separate divisions of heaven, such as purgatory, and hell? Interestingly, the original Hebrew Bible has no reference to a place called Hell. It speaks of a place beyond life called Sheol, or "the abode of the departed." Later Greek translations replaced Sheol with Hades, or Hell, referencing the god of the underworld. During the 4th Century, St. Jerome was commissioned by Pope Damasus 1 to translate the Bible to Latin and the references to Hell became standardized. Dante's 14th century epic, The Divine Comedy, gave us our modern interpretations of Heaven, Purgatory and the 9 Circles of Hell. Once again, it is the primary purpose of religions to give acceptable definition to concepts that are beyond the comprehension of the common man.

Back in college, some friends had asked me if I had ever experienced astral projection or out of body experiences. I had heard the terms but was not familiar with the practice. I went to their small upstairs apartment which was off an alley between Main Street and the college Arts building. They had me lie down on a cot and practice some breathing exercises. I was told to concentrate my total awareness on the tips of my toes and slowly move upward feeling each section, each bone and muscle, each joint of my body separately until I reached the top of my head. Then I was instructed to reverse the procedure back down to my toes. We did this several times, each time moving faster from toe to head and back.

On the last cycle I could feel my entire being rush up through me, escape through the top of my head, and float up to the ceiling of the room. It was as if I was separated from but still connected to my body. I saw my friends standing over me. I then moved higher, through the ceiling and roof. I hovered over the building and audibly described the scene to my friends. They looked out the window and confirmed every detail including the people who were walking down Main Street and were not visible to them until they passed the alleyway.

I had an even more profound experience later that year. This time it was at a concert of the Paul Winter Consort. I was sitting in the audience listening to the wonderful new age sounds of the band when my guide came to me. I felt the peaceful cold and I heard a voice that my mind's ear knew so well. She asked me if I would like to cross over and see the other side. There was no way I was going to pass up this opportunity. My energy force left my body and followed her. She took me by the hand to what appeared to be an island. It was a place that was unlike anything I could ever imagine.

All of my senses were heightened beyond my belief. The grass on the island was so green and soft I could hear it. The air was calm and clear to the point I could see it. The water was so brilliantly blue and crystalline I could taste it without touching it to my lips or tongue. Try to imagine the most incredibly beautiful place on Earth. Magnify it a million times. You're still not there. I did not want to leave. My guide, Marie, who had just revealed her name for the first time, told me that I could not stay. It was not yet my time. I was told that I had much more to do. I would impact the lives of vast numbers of people. Not until my job is done could I return.

I have repeated this practice many times since then and it has aided me greatly in my psychic sessions. Being able to leave the here and now allows me the freedom to experience the lives and messages of those who need me to connect for them. Keeping the tether to my physical body allowed me to make those jumps without losing my physical self. I always left myself a way to get back to this plane. To this day, while I am not in any rush to get there, I have no fear of death. I now understand that we are only limited by the constraints of this three dimensional plane. By stepping out of this realm we transcend time, space, and the physical senses of touch, hearing, smell, taste, and sight. We move from simply sensing to "being."

Our Choice

I have perceived a beyond which is a place of reflection and conscious decision making. In that place we are not only able to recall events and our actions of every previous lifetime but we can also see into future lives and make decisions about our next path. We can choose the situations we need to face and the lessons we need to learn. We are selecting our classes, if you will.

Although we are choosing our next path, we are not choosing the destination. You don't enter a class telling the professor what your final grade will be. We can state our intent but the outcome is fluid. Our free will is the ultimate variant in the equation of our lives. Every situation we encounter, every decision we make will impact the twists and turns that our paths will take. The test is how we handle the consequences of our actions. How often do we hear the question, "Why do bad things happen to good people?" Whether we choose to do something positive, negative or nothing at all, we are making a choice that will impact everything and everyone around us.

My first wife once told me that she was not responsible for my reaction to her actions. She was absolutely right in that my reaction was my decision. It was, however, her action that caused the situation to which I was reacting. We set up the scenario for the actions of those around us and ultimately those around each of them, and so on.

So, do we live our lives in constant fear of the exponential consequences of our actions? Not if you want to have any kind of a life. The good and positive things that we do also expand outward to impact everything and every event in the universe. The idea is that we learn from every situation, good, bad or indifferent, and apply what we learn to our future actions.

For most of us, our intention is to work toward maintaining that balance lest we risk the apocalyptic cataclysm foretold in Revelation. Keep in mind, however, that regardless of the size of the reaction, the effect is to return the forces to balance.

Chapter 3

Ghosts

Why Are They Here?

As human beings, we are conscious of the physical plane in which we carry out our daily lives. We experience it with our five primary senses. We live, we die. Those who have died and fully passed over exist on another plane. They are not bound by the constraints of those five senses. Nor are they limited by time, space, physical capability, or the lack thereof.

Between this plane and that one is another. It is sometimes called Limbo or Purgatory, and some souls are trapped here. This is where most of my work has taken place. With the aid of my guide, I make a connection between the living and those who are trapped on that middle plane.

There are groups of souls that are stuck in the middle. The first are those who have made a commitment, established a purpose, or set a goal in their life that was so firmly held that they cannot release themselves until the issue has been resolved. Second are those souls who died suddenly (as in an accident) or without their awareness (as in sleep or unconsciousness). This group is earthbound because they don't realize that they are dead.

As a medium, I also act as a healer of the spirit. My work is to help bring awareness and, if needed, closure to those who are trapped and allow them to pass over to the Ultimate Plane. I also work to bring closure to the living by delivering the messages that they need to hear in order to complete the grieving process. Notice that I said "need to hear" and not "want to hear." Healing is a necessary and sometimes painful process.

For those souls trapped by commitment, the healing is a matter of delivering the message to someone living who can continue or complete the task that holds the spirit bound. It can be as simple as saying that final goodbye, thank you, or I'm sorry; it can be as complex as finishing construction of a rocket ship that never got to be launched. Whatever the message, once it has been delivered and understood, the spirit is free to pass over. Delivering it is easy. It may take several tries to reach the understanding part.

Sometimes the messages are clouded in metaphor or symbolism. Sometimes the meaning isn't clear for days, weeks or even months. Keep in mind that time has little relevance on the other side. The important thing is that it has been delivered.

The trapped souls in the second group – those who died suddenly and may not realize they're dead – are the most troubled. These spirits may be confused, scared, angry, or frustrated. Their death may have been so violent that they just can't accept it. Imagine going up to people you know, loved ones and associates, and being completely ignored, as if you weren't even there. To them, you're not. Why can't you hear me? Can't you see me? I'm right in front of you! HEY!!!

For these souls the healing is more profound. It's necessary for me to experience the events of their death. I see it, hear it, and feel it as if I were the one who had died. If you will, I am playing back the recording of the event so that the spirit can watch it along with me. With realization comes acceptance and ultimately release.

OMG not Phillip @.
Ritual for J Restless Dead.

41

Often, when people hear strange sounds or see objects move about on their own it is merely an attempt to get their attention (and it usually works pretty well). Sometimes it's an uneasy feeling or unexplained emotion. Sometimes it can feel like a wall of energy holding us bound or keeping us out. Whatever the sensation, these are their attempts to connect with us. The task of the medium is to find out why.

It is vitally important that we, the mediums, are not influenced by the wants and expectations of our clients. This is why I try to make a point of not letting my clients tell me anything about who they hope to contact, why, when, where, or the circumstances of their death. The more information that is revealed up front by the client, the less information the spirit has to relate and the more obscure the establishing information becomes.

A friend called my wife to ask if I could do a reading for her. She blurted out the name of the person she wanted to contact which took away his opportunity to identify himself by name or gender. Just as quickly as she said his name I saw a shiny, black bicycle and a matching black helmet. When I told her about it, she began to cry. Her friend had been killed in a motorcycle accident. His bike and helmet had both been custom painted in matching shiny black. That tragic event became his best reference to identify himself.

Ghost Towns

In 1987, I had the opportunity to visit the Anasazi Indian pueblo ruins at Mesa Verde, Colorado. As a photographer it had long been a desire of mine to visit some of the sights made famous by Ansel Adams. On the morning of the trip to the mesa I awoke to a major disappointment. It was pouring down rain. Due to the elevation the clouds covered more than half of the mountain. There appeared to be little chance that I would be able to get the photographs I'd hoped for. It seemed like the entire trip might be wasted.

I reached the summit just before noon and suddenly the rain stopped. The clouds parted and I was greeted by beautiful blue sky and sunshine. It was also obvious that the rain had dampened the plans of all of the other visitors as well. My wife and son and I were the only ones there and, as such, the rangers offered to let us explore the ruins as few have done in the last 50 years. I was able to photograph the entire site without any people in the scenes. I also got to go deep into the structures and ceremonial kivas.

Archaeologists estimate that the Anasazi people emerged sometime around 1200 B.C.E., and then mysteriously vacated the Four Corners area around 1300 A.D., leaving ruins of their homes scattered throughout the area. While the reason for their disappearance is unknown, it is theorized by many archeologists that they simply blended with many of the other tribes of that region, losing their autonomy. Whatever the reason, the villages were never inhabited again. The name "Anasazi" was first applied to these pueblo tribes by archeologists in 1927 as a means of classification. It comes from the Navajo and commonly means "ancient people," "ancient ones," or more literally, "enemy ancestors." The modern Hopi use the word "Hisatsinom" in preference to Anasazi.

The Cliff Palace, Anasazi Pueblo Indian ruins
at Mesa Verde, Colorado, 1987

Many of the Native American beliefs are based in the forces of nature. Those forces live on long after the tribes have moved on or disappeared. The energy of those beliefs and rituals, and many of those who practiced them, remain in their holy places. I could feel and hear the spirits of the former inhabitants. It's the same feeling I got at the Mayan ruins in Tulum and Cozumel in Mexico. The same feelings I've experienced in The Forbidden City in Beijing, and the Great Wall of China, and old cities, towns, battlegrounds, and homes all over the world. When I stand in the midst and touch the stones, I am moved by the silent roar of hundreds and thousands of voices that no one can hear.

Remains of Mayan temple, Cozumel, Mexico

One of the palaces in the 600-year-old Forbidden City, the largest palace complex in the world. Now called the Palace Museum it covers 700,000 square meters, with nearly 800 buildings that have about 9,000 rooms in total.

When Emperor Qin Shi Huang ordered construction of the
Great Wall around 221 B.C., the labor force that built the wall
was made up largely of soldiers and convicts. It is said that as
many as 400,000 people died during the wall's construction;
many of these workers were buried within the wall itself.

The Wettest & Wickedest Town

In the summer of 2010 an old friend and former colleague of mine from the school system where I teach contacted me about a project she was undertaking and asked if I would be interested in helping. Karen C. Lilly-Bowyer had been doing extensive research on ghost stories and legends of Salisbury, NC for a newspaper column she was writing. The overwhelming response to her articles encouraged her to initiate a series of "Ghost Walk" tours similar to those in Charleston, SC and Savannah, GA. Her tours quickly became very popular. She hired assistants and scheduled more tours.

Many of the visitors asked Karen if she had a brochure or pamphlet to go along with the tours. Thus she came to me. Would I be interested in shooting some photographs of these reportedly haunted sites for a brochure? I was thrilled at the prospect. The more we worked together the more involved the project became. One year later we released our book, "The 'Wettest & Wickedest' Town - An Illustrated Guide to the Legends & Ghosts of Salisbury, North Carolina."

Most of the stories that we investigated were fairly routine. Karen researched the story and I photographed the site. Four of those sites stand out, however, in that phenomena occurred while we were there. The first was at the Wrenn House. Karen had found numerous reports of unusual activities, sounds, and physical manifestations from guests as well as employees of the restaurant. Footsteps and piano music could be heard on the upper floor, and chairs, tables, and other objects would rearrange themselves in the dining room.

I began photographing in the upstairs kitchen and pantry and then moved to the second floor dining room, ending in the main floor dining room and pub areas. I could feel the presence of entities in the building but nothing significant happened that evening. That was, until we had packed up my equipment and were heading out to my truck. I decided to stop to take a couple of nighttime shots of the exterior of the building in order to capture the dramatic sunset behind it. When I looked at the photos on my computer later that night, I noticed something that didn't seem right.

In the lower right pane of one window was a dark spot as if something were blocking the light from the large ceiling lantern inside. I enlarged the image and the face of a young girl became clearer. With a slight adjustment in the contrast the face became obvious. There were only a couple of problems with this scene, though. First of all, there were no children in the building that evening. Secondly, the window which she was peering out of was directly over a stairwell, 12 feet off the floor. I asked Karen about the girl and only then did she relate the story about her to me.

The young girl had lived in the house in the mid-1800s and it was not known how she had died. A fire had caused the roof to collapse in the early 1900s and the stairwell which had originally been on the opposite side of the room had been moved to its present location during the repairs and renovation. Where the girl stood had been floor in the 1800s.

Seeing faces in windows or other objects has long been dismissed by skeptics as Apophenia, "the imagined perception of a pattern or meaning where it does not actually exist." In this case, however, as with many others that I have encountered, the images correspond precisely with known or verifiable records. Also, the visions that I see are rarely static, as in the face of Jesus on a piece of burnt toast. They move, turn, disappear, and reappear freely while I and others watch.

A face in the window.

Interior view of the Wrenn House showing the window pane
where the face was photographed. Note the stairwell.

Pirates' Graves

Sometimes we need a little help from the other side. Karen had told me a story about three exceptionally old tombstones in a local cemetery. The local legend was that there had been three pirates who had escaped from a coastal jail and made their way inland. They became farmers and hid until someone recognized them. They were then tried and hanged, and their headstones were marked only with the skull and crossbones to identify them. Interestingly, the skull and crossbones flag was originally used by the Knights Templar, who had the world's biggest naval fleet in the 13th century and were well known for their pirate-like acts on the sea. When the Templars were forced out of France in 1312 they still had a fleet of about 18 ships. Legend has it that they took their treasure and fled to the Americas. Could these pirate graves, then, actually predate colonial America or even Columbus?

We arrived at the site just about sunset. I wanted to get some night shots of the stones to keep with the style of shots in the book. I had assumed that Karen knew where these particular headstones were. After wandering around nearly 10 acres of cemetery, Karen admitted that she didn't know the "specific" location of the graves. It was now pitch-black night and I only had one small flashlight with weak batteries to help guide us. I suggested that we come back the next day, in the daylight, to mark the location and then wait until dark to get the shots. Before we left I asked her to describe the stones to me one more time. She said that they were about 18" tall, rounded top, very old and weathered, in a row of three across. Looking down, we were standing directly on top of the graves. I got the shots that night.

I believe that I was meant to get the photographs in order to help tell their story and we were led to the graves to make that happen.

A "pirate's" tombstone. Salisbury, NC.

Graveyard Mystery

Often, when I am presented with a mystery, a message, or a vision, I am intrigued enough to delve into research in order to authenticate the person or event. In 1977 I got married for the first time (that's a long story for another book). At the wedding reception my good friend and best man, Walter Cook, came up to me with a very interesting discovery that a friend of his had found. Off in a remote corner of a local cemetery, behind a bush, was a small headstone. It was a granite marker, about 24" tall by 14" wide by 2½" thick and very weathered. She told me about the date of birth on the stone and I was immediately intrigued. It hadn't occurred yet. There was no visible date of death.

I made my excuses to the guests, grabbed my camera, and left for the cemetery. She took me to the spot where the headstone was standing. At first I couldn't see it behind the bush. We bent the bush aside and there it was. A single name was engraved, "JENNEIRICOTA." The date of birth on the stone was Oct. 8, 1977. That day's date was August 7, 1977. It did look as though the stone had been broken close to the ground at one time and the date of death (which appears to also be in October) was half buried and the year was not visible. I took several photographs of the stone and the surrounding area and returned to the wedding reception with a new mystery to solve. What a great wedding present!

I began my search at City Hall where I had four copies of an 8x10 black and white print of the tombstone photograph, dated and notarized on September 8, 1977 for future verification purposes. I'm quite sure that it was a first for the Notary Public. Walter has one of the copies, Dr. DeChenne, the professor of Parapsychology at SUNY Geneseo, has another, and I have two. At the County Clerk's office, I looked up every possible combination and division of the name that I could devise. I looked for last names under Cota, Ricota, Neiricota, and Jenneiricota, along with any possible given name that could come close to fitting. I looked at 1977, 1971, 1917, and 1911 in case there was any stylizing in the engraving of the numbers. All of the combinations came up empty.

The Clerk directed me to the Catholic Church across the street. It was their cemetery and they would have records of all burials there. The Pastor was unavailable but the housekeeper offered to help. They had a large map of the entire cemetery which divided it into numbered sections with each grave marked and labeled. The entry for this plot was assigned to "Ricotta, lot 30." We went to the file cabinet to find the folder with the information for this specific plot and it was empty. It seemed that I was hitting one dead end after another (pun intended), and the date on the stone was fast approaching.

My next stop took me to the local funeral home. Being a small village of less than 7,000 residents, there weren't too many funeral homes to choose from. I was told by the director that this was indeed the home that serviced that cemetery. Unfortunately, his records only went back to 1968 when he purchased the business. We located the former owner's widow and asked her if she had any knowledge of the records of the funeral home. She assumed that they had all been either lost or destroyed in the transfer of the business.

On October 7th, the day before the engraved date of birth, Walt and I had decided to make one more visit to the County Clerk's office. A woman in the office told us about a Mr. Joseph Ricotta who was the local Postmaster. We rushed over to the Post Office to find Mr. Ricotta. He told me that the stone belonged to a sister of his who had died as a young girl around 1925. Her name was Genevive (Jennei) Ricotta and she was born in 1911. The stone had been carved by his older brother, Anthony, who was not an experienced stone cutter. He had to drop letters from the name because he started too large and realized that they would not all fit. He tried to be fancy with the "1s" but they came out looking like "7s." It all seemed to easily solve the mysteries. Perhaps too easily.

Many questions were left unanswered. Why was the stone left uncared for by the family so that it was hidden by the large bush? If the brother's attempt at adding serifs to the "1s" made them look like "7s" why didn't he do the same with the "1" at the start of 1977? Why was the date of death hidden? Why was the file folder at the church empty? Why were there no records of the child's birth or death at the County Hall? Did the Postmaster solve the mystery or just offer a convenient way to end the search?

Photograph of a headstone, notarized one month
before the inscribed date of birth.

Chapter 4

Earthbound Because They Don't Know That They Are Dead

Helping One Pass Over

A girl I dated in college had a friend from her home town, Hans. He rode the coolest metal-flake blue, tear drop tank, extended fork, Honda 750 chopper you've ever seen. She was from a very well-to-do family in the Albany area and, as rebellious teens are prone to do, only dated hippies and bikers (I was the former and Hans the latter). One night around midnight, they decided to take a cruise on the bike and headed out on the highway. As fate would have it, a group of under-aged girls were out partying and went for a midnight drive in the country. The driver of the car did not see the headlight of the motorcycle when she ran the stop sign. Hans locked the brakes and skidded the bike into the driver's door of the car. The girlfriend was thrown from the bike and suffered broken fingers, teeth, left leg, and several vertebrae. She was the lucky one. Hans stayed with the bike. The gas tank burst into flames as it slid across the pavement. By the time it hit the car, the bike and Hans were fully engulfed. Hans had massive skull fractures. He had third degree burns over 95% of his body but due to the brain damage never regained consciousness. He died the next afternoon in the hospital.

A few months later I had the honor to meet and work with Ed and Lorraine Warren. They are the husband and wife team that did the original investigations into the Amityville House on Long Island, NY, on which the book and movie were based. While working with Ed and Lorraine I had several psychic experiences and they classified me as a "deep trance medium" due to the way I would completely separate from the present during the contacts.

During one of our sessions I was suddenly overcome with intense pain all over my body, and it felt like I was having the worst migraine of my life. At the same time, I could feel the enveloping cold and peaceful calm of my guide as she rushed in to protect me. I was crying profusely and began to scream out, "It hurts. It burns. My God, make it stop burning," over and over. I knew immediately that it was Hans. Ed and Lorraine could see the fear and confusion he displayed through me. Lorraine immediately recognized that he was one of those entities who did not know that he was dead. She began to reassure him that everything would be all right. She told him that he was now dead and it was time to pass over. With that, he completed his transition.

Transitioning

On Saturday, March 18, 1989, I received a very stressful call from my mother. I was living in North Carolina and she and my step-father were living in Florida. She told me that Sheldon was very ill and that I might want to come down there soon. I could tell by the tone of her voice that soon meant immediately.

My mother remarried when I was 16 and it was, to say the least, not easy for me to accept a father figure into my life at that time. He was a stern disciplinarian which made matters worse. We got off to a rocky start, but after some very heated confrontations we realized that we needed to learn to be friends before we could ever be father and son. Sheldon was a mechanical engineer and pioneer in the field of fiber optics. He taught me many things when it came to building, repairing, and problem solving. As the years passed I grew to admire his intelligence in things technical, accept his awkwardness in things familial, and appreciate his love and devotion for my mother.

That Monday, Mom and I took him to the dialysis center for his weekly treatment. Sheldon suffered from advanced kidney failure complicated by emphysema while he continued to smoke at least two packs a day. Due to his weakened state, the nurses were unable to find a viable vein. The doctor took my mother and me into a private room to discuss the options. He could be taken to the hospital to wait out the end or we could take him home.

What must go through a person's mind when they know that the end of their life is imminent? We had time to talk about many things during those last few days. I held him in my arms and helped ease his transition as he died on that Friday morning, his 81st birthday.

The conscious awareness and acceptance of our dying ensures our full passing to the other side. Hospice care gives the terminally ill an opportunity to bring closure to this life, whether physically, emotionally, financially, or spiritually. As a Healing Touch Practitioner, my wife Betz helps those in transition calmly and easily pass. When there is a smooth transition, those who have passed know that they can return to visit or assist those still living whenever there is a need. Sheldon is not earthbound. He returns whenever he is called on to help find misplaced objects and answer questions. He is always welcome if for nothing else than just to be there from time to time.

Sheldon Rex Gee (1976)

Battlefields and Cemeteries

I have photographed several cemeteries over the years and had some interesting experiences in each one. Often, I am asked if I avoid cemeteries because of all of the people buried there. Actually, most of them are very quiet places. Only the remains of the bodies are there, not the souls. Typically, spirits tend to remain where they lived or died, not where they are buried. The Battle of Guilford Courthouse, 1781, was the largest, most hotly-contested battle of the Revolutionary War's Southern Campaign. Nearly 4500 colonists under Major General Nathanael Greene and 1900 British troops under Lord Charles Cornwallis fought for 2 ½ hours until Greene's troops finally retreated, leaving almost ¼ of all dead. Located in what is now Greensboro, NC, for me the site rings with the sounds of the dead and dying. Likewise, it is difficult for me to drive past the Appomattox Courthouse Civil War battle site in Virginia. While nearly 90,000 troops were involved, amazingly only about 1200 were killed between Grant's and Lee's forces. Outnumbered more than 2:1, Lee chose to surrender rather than face certain devastating losses.

Graveyards do work as a focus point for the living when they are trying to connect with specific persons. Many people believe that if they go to the grave of a deceased loved one that they can talk to them and be heard. The reality is that the loved one can hear you wherever you are. It's your thinking of them that opens the connection.

The National Cemetery in Salisbury, NC is an exception to this rule. I found this site to be extremely noisy. The cemetery was located only a couple of miles from a Confederate prison camp. The number of Union soldiers being held there was so great that when they died, either from their wounds or the conditions in the camp, they were buried in mass, trench graves with only a general marker identifying the grave as "Union." There were several of these trenches and in them thousands of soldiers were buried, layer upon layer. Tragically, many of the soldiers who were buried weren't quite dead when they were interred. I could not stay long at this site as the moans and wails and pleas for help were overwhelming.

Markers identifying the trench graves of Union soldiers
at the National Cemetery, Salisbury, NC.

"Look, Look!"

Sometimes the visions that I see and the messages I hear are metaphoric or symbolic. My wife, Betz, and I were invited to do a reading at the home of a friend in the town of Spencer, NC. Upon entering the house, I immediately felt recognition. The friend had a coat rack that was made of old metal door knobs hanging in the entry way but I saw an older, larger glass doorknob in my mind. As the session began I felt the presence of an older gentleman who had lived there and may have been the builder of the house. I sensed he would open and close the door to the front room and walk about to make sure all was right throughout the house.

He was very happy with the current owner and her care of the house. However, he wanted to know if she was going to rehang the kitchen door, the one with the large glass doorknob. He also told her to be wary of an event that was coming up the next day between 1:00 and 3:00.

I next saw a little girl of about five or six years of age. She was wearing a dark blue or black dress with a strawflower print and lace trim, but no shoes. The girl stood at the top of the stairs and called for me to "Come, come see, quickly, come! Look! Look!" She ran down the hallway to the left of the stairs, to a front room. In my mind's eye, I followed her down the hall. The room was on the right of the hall. There was one bed with a white comforter. A small desk or dressing table was near the window. There were woven baskets near the bed and the girl was pointing excitedly under the bed. She kept repeating, "Look! Look! LOOK!"

Finally, I felt the presence of a third entity. I couldn't tell gender but the letter "M" was prevalent. This entity could not speak in words, though it tried very hard. I could feel my mouth open and close as if to speak but no words came out. "Mmmmmm, mmmmm, mmmmm" was all it could say. I had a profound feeling of love and caring and that this entity really missed the homeowner.

When the session ended I could see that our friend was emotionally shaken. She said that the door to the front room would constantly open when no one was around. She and her daughter would hear footsteps and then find that the door they had closed only moments before was again open. We also learned that the current owner was planning to meet with buyers for the house the next afternoon, and that the door for the kitchen had been removed and was in the basement.

I asked about the "M" and someone who couldn't speak. That's when she began to cry. Unbeknownst to me, she had earlier told Betz that she had hoped to hear from her dog "Missy" who had passed and whom she missed dearly. I have often been asked if I can contact pets that have passed. When we see a movement in the corner of our eye and then turn to see nothing there at all, was it the spirit of someone or something? Could it have been the cat we loved so dearly or the dog who had been by our side when we were young? Skeptics will tell us that it was merely the fluid moving around the eyeball catching a glimmer of light on the edges of our peripheral vision. This glancing image triggers memories which we then associate with what we want it to be. Perhaps. But, what if it was someone else who saw the movement and then related to you details that only you knew prior to that moment?

Do animals have sentient souls? From time to time, I have seen cats, dogs or other animals in my visions, but I never saw them as anything more than references to the life of the person who had passed. They were like a familiar possession to help identify the entity. This was different. Missy was, indeed, trying to communicate.

We know that we can talk to our animals and train them to respond to specific commands and routines. Pet psychics, and outstanding pet trainers like Cesar Milan the "Dog Whisperer," are said to possess animal telepathy, or the ability to communicate mentally with animals. But do animals really possess the level of understanding that we refer to as sentience?

Historically, most Biblical scholars have adamantly denied the existence of a soul in animals, citing Genesis 1:26 in which God says, *"Let us make man in our image, in our likeness, and let them rule over the fish of the sea and the birds of the air, over the livestock, over all the earth, and over all the creatures that move along the ground."* However, in 1990, Pope John Paul II stated publically that, *"animals, like men, were given the 'breath of life' by God."* In fact, the word "animal" is derived from the Greek word 'anima' meaning psyche or soul. Various religions and philosophies hold differing views on the subject. The Hindus believe that we have all evolved through reincarnation throughout every stage of plant and animal life. While the Jews and Methodists hold that though all living things have souls, they are each at their own level of intellectual hierarchy in the eyes of God. They believe that only man can possess a sentient soul.

As I receive more messages and communications from animals who were close to their "owners," I am convinced that they possess a much higher level of awareness than mankind has attributed to them. I do believe that we can learn a lot from them, if we take the time to listen.

After the session, I asked our friend if we could go upstairs to see what the little girl had shown me. The first thing I noticed was that the stairs and hallway were on the opposite side of my vision. We walked down the hall and the room on the right was not the room I had seen. The room on the left, however, had one bed with a white comforter. There was a small dressing table by the window and a woven basket stand was next to the bed.

I looked under the bed as the girl had insisted. Under some plastic storage boxes was a large, old mirror, a "looking glass." Everything I had seen had been a mirror image. The little girl had died from a childhood illness and was one of those spirits who didn't know she was dead. She couldn't understand why no one could see or hear her. When she realized I saw her, she was so excited! She had to show me around her house.

This had been a great day of healing. We helped the old man know that his house would be taken care of. The little girl could accept her passing, and the homeowner had a chance to reunite with her beloved dog and say goodbye. The homeowner has told us that since that afternoon there has been no more activity in the house. The door stays closed and all is quiet. They have all moved on.

Chapter 5

Earthbound Because They Have Unfinished Business

Delivering a Message

I was home from college for a Thanksgiving weekend and the entire family (mom, step-dad, younger sister, older sister, step-sister, and nephew) were all together in the house. There were only three bedrooms so I agreed to give my room up to my step-sister and her three-year-old son and sleep on the sofa in the sunroom.

After dinner, my step-sister and I were in the sunroom talking about who-knows-what when I suddenly saw her bathed in a soft blue light with the exception of a patch of red at her throat. While I had heard about auras, I'd not seen them before, and this one was quite vivid. Auras are generally defined, either spiritually or scientifically, as emanations of the electromagnetic field surrounding a person, animal, or object. Kirlian photography can actually capture images of these fields and the disturbances in them that may normally be unseen by the human eye. I asked her if she had any problems with her throat recently and she revealed that she was just getting over a severe strep infection.

Within a few minutes of talking to my step-sister, I felt a presence in the south end of the room near the ceiling. She said that she had felt like something had been following her. There were two entities, both female, one older than us and the other older than the first. It quickly became clear to me from comments and facts that I was now relating to my step-sister (all of which had occurred long before I met her and none of which I had any way of knowing) that they were her mother and grandmother. Her mother died following a brief illness when my step-sister was a teenager. I felt that the two were traveling together to protect my step-sister and to deliver an important message.

The wall opposite the windows in the room was covered with shelves of books belonging to both my mother and step-father. I was drawn to run my hand across one specific shelf. When I came to a particular book it felt ice cold. I pulled the book from the shelf and my step-sister immediately gave an audible gasp. It was her mother's favorite book of poetry. Her father had placed the book on the shelf along with many of his other books and I had not noticed it before that night. I ran my fingers down the contents page until I came to a title that made me burst into tears. Opening the book to that page I read the poem aloud. Unlike rhapsodomancy, or prophetic verse, in which verses are selected at random and then divined for guidance, this poem was not chosen by chance. I was deliberately guided to it.

After I finished reading, my step-sister told me that she and her mother had a terrible argument on the night before her mother died and that it had not been resolved. The poem, entitled *"The Absent Ones,"* by Charles M. Dickinson (1842–1924), was a message from her mother telling her she regretted never getting to say "I'm sorry and I miss you."

"The Absent Ones,"

"I shall leave the old house in Autumn,
To traverse its threshold no more;
Ah! How shall I sigh for the dear ones,

That meet me each morn at the door!
I shall miss the 'goodnights' and the kisses,
And the gush of their innocent glee,
The group on its green, and the flowers,
That are brought every morning to me.

I shall miss them at morn and at even,
Their song in the school and the street;
I shall miss the low hum of their voices,
And the tread of their delicate feet.
When the lessons of life are all ended,
And death says, 'The school is dismissed!'
May the little ones gather around me.
To bid me good night and be kissed!"

I replaced the book in its space on the shelf and spent the night in the room alone. While I may not be the lightest sleeper, sudden noises or movements in a room will instantly awaken me. No one entered the room that night. The next morning the book had been moved to the end of the shelf and my stepsister's family bible was in its place. The message had been delivered and the entities moved on.

Fulfilling a Promise

I had met a young woman from Israel, D, in one of my art classes who asked me if I would like her to do a Tarot reading for me. I had never had a Tarot reading before this and was quite curious to see what she would discover. Her reading was quite astounding. She told me that I had abilities to speak with the dead and know things otherwise unknown. I couldn't argue with her on those points. She then asked me if I would come to her apartment to meet her husband and discuss a problem they had been experiencing.

At the apartment I met her husband, M. D was born in Bethlehem, Israel and met M, who was from New York, while he served in the Israeli Air Force. After his service was up, they moved to the Rochester area to attend college. They explained to me that they had been experiencing a strange feeling in the apartment, as if there were a heavy cloud that would try to hold them there or block them from leaving. They asked me if I could try to sense something and see what I could do to help them.

I didn't feel anything that evening. After dinner, I agreed to spend the night on the living room sofa and, if nothing happened, return to campus in the morning. That night, all was quiet and uneventful. The next morning, however, was anything but. As we prepared to leave the apartment I could feel the presence she had described. It was as if a wall of energy was blocking the door. I called for my guide and she wrapped me in her cold, protective cloak. I told the couple to sit with me on the floor of the kitchen. I carefully instructed them not to touch me, speak to me, answer any questions, or make any sounds or gestures that might influence what was about to happen. It is essential that we let whatever is to happen, happen on its own.

Often we hear about people called "cold readers" who can pick up on the reactions of people around them to craft responses that seem "divine." The Amazing Kreskin, who was famous for his ESP skills, referred to himself as a "mentalist" not a psychic. He would pay careful attention to the person's responses to key words and phrases. Even minute reactions, such as eyebrow twitches, blinking, breathing changes, and flushing of the face would give him the clues he needed to direct his next statement. By specifically directing the people around me to avoid any physical, visual, or audible response or reaction, I try to dispel any inference of influence. If my reading is off base or totally wrong, let it be. That makes it all the much more valid when it is accurate.

Almost as soon as I had given the couple their instructions I was "gone." I looked down at myself and could see that I was tall, almost 6'4". I had blonde wavy hair and large, very muscular hands. I was wearing a tan colored, short sleeved shirt with shoulder epaulets. My tan pants were tucked neatly into my black boots. I was running down a dirt road in a small desert village. The houses on either side of the road looked like sandstone cubes with openings cut out for windows and doors. At the end of the street was a vast expanse of sun-scorched desert, stretching for miles and ending at the base of snowcapped mountains. I remember thinking to myself that I had never seen a sight quite like that before.

As I ran down the dirt street, I felt a searing pain tear through the back of my left shoulder. I grasped with my right hand at the site of the wound as I fell, face forward, into the dirt. Suddenly, I was entering a house. On the wall to the right of the hallway was a small, half round table with a lace doily over the top of it. I walked down the hallway to a bedroom. To my right was a window. Through it I could see that the house was high on the side of a hill overlooking a body of water. In front of me was a four poster bed with lace sheers gathered at each post, ready to be drawn to keep the insects away through the night. There was an embroidered tapestry hanging on the wall over the head of the bed.

Finally, I was on the top of a mountain with D. I reached down and picked a small yellow rose and handed it to her saying, "You are my little flower, my little sister. I will be back to see you as soon as I have finished."

And it was over. What had seemed like a matter of minutes had, in fact, lasted nearly two hours. I was physically and emotionally exhausted. Both D and M were in tears. They told me that I had repeatedly said the name "Jawrj" or George. That was the name of D's cousin. He had been a tank commander in the Israeli Army and was shot in the back while trying to escape enemy forces in the Golan Heights in a village just like the one I described. It was in the summer and he was wearing the summer uniform. He was an unusual man for an Israeli in that he was tall with blonde wavy hair, and he was a sculptor with very strong hands. The house I had described was D's home in Bethlehem. From her bedroom window you could see the Dead Sea.

On the afternoon before he was deployed to the Golan, George met D on a hill near her home and gave her the little yellow rose with the promise to return. What I had not been aware of during the session was that I had also recited a prayer. It was the prayer of the kibbutz that George had been raised in. Only members of a kibbutz are allowed to recite their prayer. D had heard George pray this many times and knew it well. What made it even more interesting was that I recited it in fluent Hebrew. Xenoglossy occurs when a medium is in communication with the spirit of a dead person and speaks in a language of which they are unfamiliar. While I had learned some Yiddish growing up in New York, I do not speak Hebrew and I have never been to the Middle East. At that time there were no longer any surviving members George's kibbutz.

After the session, the veil had lifted. The couple never again felt the wall of energy holding them. On this day George had finally fulfilled his promise.

Waiting for the Return

The Empire Hotel in downtown Salisbury, NC has been a landmark since it first opened in 1859. It remained in operation until the 1960s and has many stories connected to it. While doing the photography and research for the book on the Salisbury hauntings, I had the opportunity to observe a group of paranormal investigators conducting a thorough sweep of the building. It was fascinating to watch them with their EMF meters, full spectrum cameras, EVP recorders, tri-field meters, laser grids, and more.

Electromagnetic field, or EMF, meters emit a loud audible alarm when they encounter any disturbance in the field. Tri-field meters read a combination of magnetic, electric, and analog radio/microwaves. They can be influenced by anomalies in the house such as poorly grounded wires, dimmer switches, and computers. The Empire had been vacant for over 50 years and there were no electrical connections that would cause any interference.

Full spectrum cameras are capable of capturing images in nonvisible ultraviolet and infrared, as well as visible red, green, and blue (or what we refer to as white) wavelengths. Laser grids project a pattern against a wall or light up a room, and if something passes in front of it, it will block out sections of the grid. These are used for detecting movement, shadows, or solid shapes moving in the room but can only be used effectively for about 10 minutes at a time or they risk overheating.

The process of electronic voice phenomena, or EVP, recording was first introduced into paranormal research by Dr. Konstantin Raudive, a Latvian born psychologist, in 1971. Enthusiasts of the use of EVP recorders claim that they enable the dead to communicate within the electronic field of digital or analog recordings. Usually the recordings have to be subjected to amplification and filtering to render clearly audible words. EVPs are divided into three categories:

- Class A: Easily understood by almost anyone with little or no dispute. These are also usually the loudest EVPs.
- Class B: Usually characterized by warping of the voice in certain syllables. Lower in volume or more distant sounding than Class A. Class B is the most common type of EVP.
- Class C: Characterized by excessive warping. They are the lowest in volume (often whispering) and are the hardest to understand.

The idea of such devices date back to Thomas Edison who was quoted in the October 1920 issue of *Scientific America* magazine,

> "I don't claim that our personalities pass on to another existence or sphere. I don't claim anything because I don't know anything about the subject. For that matter, no human being knows. But I do claim that it is possible to construct an apparatus which will be so delicate that if there are personalities in another

existence or sphere who wish to get in touch with us in this existence or sphere, the apparatus will at least give them a better opportunity to express themselves than the tilting tables and raps and Ouija boards and mediums and other crude methods now purported to be the only means of communication."

While I may take slight umbrage at having mediums lumped in with "crude methods," it was obvious that Edison, Tesla, and many noted scientists and inventors of that period had a great deal of interest in all things occult.

Skeptics claim that listeners are simply hearing what they hope to hear, creating words in the noise that aren't actually there. The phenomenon is called "Pareidolia," a subset of Apophenia which applies to finding meaning in sound or images that does not exist. Psychologists explain this as a way for the mind to create some semblance of order out of chaos. They classify Apophenia into the five Gestalt Laws of Perceptual Organization. They include:

The Law of Similarity: Similar stimuli or elements that are close together tend to be grouped.

The Law of Closure: Stimuli tend to be grouped into complete figures.

The Law of Good Continuation: Stimuli tend to be grouped so as to minimize change or discontinuity.

The Law of Symmetry: Regions bound by symmetrical borders tend to be perceived as coherent figures.

The Law of Simplicity: Ambiguous stimuli tend to be resolved in favor of the simplest.

This is why it is necessary for paranormal investigators to use a variety of methods to detect and record phenomena. Any single method can be refuted as coincidental or inferential. When multiple modes are utilized and give corroborating evidence, it is harder to pass the experience off as someone's imagination.

The group was just finishing their investigation of one of the second floor hallways where they had detected some activity. They began audibly asking questions into the hallway to see if they could elicit a response. When they asked if the entity had come to the hotel in order to hide an affair with a mistress, I got the feeling of boisterous laughter, though none was to be heard aloud.

As the team left the corridor, I stayed behind and asked one of the investigators to wait with me for a moment. All at once, I was enveloped by a bone chilling cold. It was August and the old building had no cooling or ventilation of any kind. It was over 100°F in the hallway. Tears began to run down my face. I asked the researcher to place her hand near my back and arms but not to touch me at all. She felt the cold radiating all around me.

I felt the presence of an older African-American gentleman. Unlike the clips of words or short phrases perceived in the EVP recordings, I could clearly hear this man's voice in full coherent sentences. His called himself Mr. Josiah. He had been the son of freed slaves who got a job working at the hotel around the turn of the 20th century. Mr. Josiah lived in a room in the basement level of the hotel, which, I later found out, is where all of the servant staff lived.

When he was asked by the researchers if he had come to the hotel to carry on an affair behind his wife's back he roared with laughter. He had never married. This hallway had been his charge. All of the guests were his family and he made their comfort his life's priority. He conveyed to me that he was staying at the hotel in hopes that it would someday be renovated and restored to original grandeur. He is waiting for his "family" to return.

Second floor hallway in the Empire Hotel.

Righting a Wrong

It was the summer of 1973 and I had just graduated from high school. My girlfriend and I, along with two of our best friends, went out to dinner at a lovely little restored Civil War era inn called Webber's Wayside Inn Restaurant, in Elbridge, NY. While we were eating I turned to our male friend and commented that the restaurant was haunted. He said that he thought he had felt something strange as well. Our girlfriends thought it was "cool" to have a "real live ghost" in the room. I had to point out that ghosts are no longer "live," at least by our standards. Our male friend accompanied me to the hostess station where I asked to speak to a manager. When she arrived she was a bit taken aback by my first question. "Is this inn haunted?" Obviously curious, she asked me why I would ask that question.

I told her that I had sensed a woman in her early twenties. In my mind's eye, I could see her, dressed in a beautiful yellow and white, Civil War era formal dress with hoop skirt and layers of petticoats. Her brown hair is meticulously set in long flowing curls. She comes down the main staircase from one of the rooms on an upper floor only to see her fiancé, freshly returned from the war and in his finest officer's dress uniform, dancing with another woman. She promptly turns around, runs back upstairs to her room and hangs herself. With that, the manager took us aside and told us about the woman and how she still haunts the inn to this day.

Many of her employees have reported seeing sugar bowls or salt and pepper shakers fly across the room as if thrown in rage. Footsteps running up and down the stairs, tables and chairs rearranged and place settings being shuffled are common occurrences. The manager's last question to me was, "How did you know?" I just saw it all happening as I sat there. It wasn't as if I had been told about it. I truly experienced the events of that evening in the summer of 1865.

In June of 2013, Betz and I drove to Elbridge, NY, to the inn where I had experienced the spirit presence over 40 years earlier. The building today is the "Wayside Irish Pub." I went inside the pub and asked the young lady behind the bar if she was the owner. She explained the she was not but that the owner would be back later in the day. I introduced myself as a photographer from North Carolina, working on a book about haunted places around the country. She stopped what she was doing to immediately call her mother, the owner.

Margo Spain, the young woman's mother, wasted little time coming directly to the pub. I introduced myself and told her about a book I had released on the hauntings in Salisbury, NC and about my experiences in her building so many years ago. Margo told me that there had been several psychics and paranormal investigators who had come to the building during the time she has been there, and all reported nearly identical impressions. I asked her if we could tour the building and take some pictures, and she eagerly agreed.

The Wayside Irish Pub, Elbridge, NY. The arrow
indicates the room where a young woman died.

We went first to the room that was originally the main
floor ballroom and dining room. This was the room where
I had sensed the young woman from the Civil War era. The
feelings were still very strong. I asked if we could go upstairs
and again Margo readily agreed. Before we started up the stairs
I took a photograph which immediately showed two distinct
orbs against a very dark wood banding strip.

The main stairway to the second floor of the Wayside Irish Pub.
Two disinct orbs appered as we began to climb the stairs.

When we got to the top of the stairs the presence was overwhelming. The girl in the yellow dress was there to greet me once again.

Since Margo was telling me about the experiences she and her staff had in these rooms, I felt it was safe for me to tell her I was a medium. She was not the least bit surprised. She showed me the rooms on the second floor and I could feel the presence of the girl. I asked Margo if we could go up to the third floor. She removed the velvet rope from the stair rail that was intended to deter workers from going up there and led the way. At the top of the stairs I again began taking photographs and went room to room until I came to the room in the southeast corner of the building. The feeling in that room was that of frustration and desperation. I received strong and vivid impression of the events of that night. The girl had not just happened to see her man dancing with another woman. The affair had been going on for some time and now he was flaunting it publicly. The girl felt that she had no choice but to make the world know how she had been deceived. She went to her room and took off the yellow dress that she'd had made specifically for this occasion. She had intended that evening to tell her fiancé that she was pregnant with his child. I believe that the two orbs that we saw on the stairs were the young woman and her child.

She carefully and methodically put her gown on the dress mannequin, removed the long yellow ribbons which tied the waist and draped down the back of the skirt, and stared at the ribbons in her hands for several minutes. She used those ribbons to hang herself from a ceiling rafter. I could see her hanging, dressed only in her white petticoat. Her head was turned with her chin on her right shoulder and her long dark hair framing her face.

On this day the room was bare. At some point an acoustic tile ceiling had been applied over the rafters, the walls were paneled, a closet was added, and it bore little resemblance to the original room I had perceived.

The room where the young woman died has been rebuilt and remodeled
several times. Originally it had an exposed rafter ceiling, no closet,
and papered walls. She was found hanging just inside the door.

We made our way back down to the main floor and just as we reached the bottom of the stairs we heard a loud crash. I looked up to see a white rectangle bounce at the top of the stairs. I went up to see what it was and found that the front of the EXIT sign above the stairs had been pried loose from its frame and dropped (rather forcefully) to the floor below. I often ask the entities for a sign that they acknowledge my contact, but this was literal. That it was an "EXIT" sign could be taken as a demand for us to leave. On this day, however, there was absolutely no feeling of ill will. I readily caught the humor of the sign reference and thanked the entity for responding. I promised her that I would tell her story.

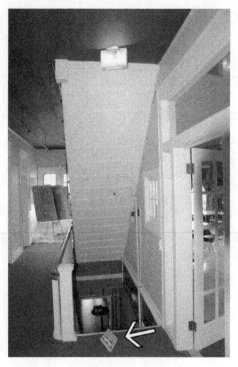

I asked for a "sign."

Although Margo was no stranger to unusual phenomena in the pub, she was visibly shaken by the thrown sign. I assured her that the entity was not malicious or physically harmful. While she will continue to make herself known through noises, apparitions, and moving objects, she had no intention of harming any living being.

Upon returning to North Carolina I started to do some research into the historic structure. It was originally built in 1830 by Squire Munroe as an inn to serve passengers on the Jordan & Skaneateles stagecoach lines. First called the Munroe House, it provided rooming accommodations for the whopping fee of $1.50 a day. Historical newspaper accounts from the Jordan and Elbridge area reported a couple different young ladies who died in the late summer of 1865. The causes of the deaths were not reported, only that they had "died at home." Could one of those have been the family's way of keeping the secret of the pregnancy and suicide?

In 1913 the building was almost completely destroyed in a terrible fire. Two years later, the inn was rebuilt in the original Italianate design. While the appearance was similar to the original, there were many "upgrades" throughout the structure. That explained why the room where the young woman died, while the same overall size and location in the building, looked so different than what was shown to me in my vision of the events on that evening in 1865. In 1941, the then Cross Keys Inn was sold and renamed the Wayside Inn. In 1960, there was another fire that damaged the building. The building was sold to Frederick Weber in 1967. Weber renamed the restaurant

Weber's Wayside Inn. This historic building has also been known as the Elbridge Inn and Smart's Wayside Inn. Today it is the Wayside Irish Pub.

Historic photograph of the original Munroe House ca.1835.

Sometimes I will receive messages and details hours or days after the initial encounter. These help to fill in some of the blanks. In this case, the rest of the story came 40 years after I first sensed the entity. The young girl could not rest until her story was made known, keeping in mind that time has no bearing on those who have passed. Her whole story is now posted behind the bar at the inn so that everyone can know what really happened.

An Urgent Request

One morning, while Betz was doing her morning meditation, she felt the presence of an entity she was not familiar with. It was not her mother or one of her healing spirits but something else. She asked me to see if I could feel anything.

We went into Betz' in-home healing room and began a session. The spirit moved quickly, with an urgency that I don't often feel. Almost immediately, I was standing in front of a house in the Salisbury area. It was an old, Victorian home with a wide set of five steps to the front porch. Straight back from the top of the stairs was a double door. The wooden doors had oval window panels on the top half; the door on the right had an old twist-type doorbell centered just below the window.

As I entered the house, there was a stairway to my right going up to the second floor and a hallway straight ahead. The hall led first to the dining room with a large table in the center and a sideboard next to a small fireplace on the wall shared with the kitchen. The kitchen had been remodeled but retained an old, bulky, butcher-block island and the large white farm type kitchen sink.

The entity was very upset. He had a sense of urgency in his message. "The book, the book, have to find the book, have to finish it..." He was a writer, perhaps for a newspaper or of journals. Although he had an office on the second floor, he preferred to do his writing at the dining room table, with his back to the kitchen. Somewhere in the house is a journal or notebook that contains what he considered to be his greatest work. He is trying to get a message to anyone who can possibly find his book.

He knew Betz from her work as a marketing and promotions director in Salisbury. I could see him watch her as she walked down Main Street past the shops she used to frequent. We still don't know what his connection to her was or when, but we are keeping the connection open. If I have learned anything along this path, it is that the answers will manifest themselves when the time is right. Never try to read into what we see. Just let it happen as it needs to.

Almost six months passed when Betz and I stopped to deliver some promotional materials to a friend of hers in Salisbury. We only had a few minutes to meet her in a corner parking lot as she was on her way to another appointment. She mentioned that she recently had some feelings of tension and anxiety in her house and wondered if I might come by some day to check it out.

As it was, the house was just on the other side of a tall hedge from the parking lot and I couldn't resist taking a quick look. When I came around the hedge, I froze. I called out for Betz to come quickly. It was the house I had seen in the vision, right down to the old fashioned, twist-type doorbell. The homeowner has not yet invited us in to find the journal and resolve the entity's unfinished business, but we are eagerly anticipating the opportunity.

As I had mentioned in the account of the Wayside Inn, time is only a constraint for our plane of existence. We get to things according to our perceived order of importance. For those on the other side, time has no meaning.

If we come back tomorrow or in ten years, the now is still the now. I do promise, however, that when we do investigate the mystery of the journal I will give a full account. I do have to leave something for future books, after all.

Chapter 6

Earthbound or Returned Because They Feel a Sense of Responsibility

Penny's House

In 2006, I met and eventually married my current (and, if it please the gods, last) wife, Betz McKeown. She has been the most supportive and inspirational partner anyone could ever hope for.

In 2010, Betz's mother, Penny, died shortly after being diagnosed with stage IV colon cancer. While her mom was in Hospice care, Betz was introduced to Healing Touch. Healing Touch is one of the many powers of the mind and spirit that I mentioned earlier. The Bible calls it the "Laying on of Hands," and refers to it 42 times in the New Testament alone. She saw how effectively it calmed the fear and pain of the Hospice patients and how beautifully it eased their transition from this plane to the next. Betz was so moved by the experience that she went on to study the healing art, receive her international certification, and open her own practice in Winston-Salem, NC.

Shortly after Penny died we took over her property in Asheville and decided to fix it up for rental. Along with the usual painting and cleaning there was a long list of repairs and replacements that needed to be done before it would be ready for tenants. Among those was the replacement and rewiring of every electrical outlet and light switch in the house.

Penny's House, Asheville, NC

While the main electric service and much of the main wiring had been replaced when her mom was living, the old, ungrounded, two pronged, outlets remained. It took about two days to replace all of the receptacles but, after testing each one as I went and being satisfied with my work, the task was deemed finished and we were ready for bed. Or so I thought.

As we were getting under the covers on the inflatable bed we had set up in the living room, I reached to turn on a small lamp on the floor nearby. Click and nothing happened. I checked the bulb, tried another lamp, still nothing. I plugged my outlet tester in and, sure enough, there was no power to the outlet. It was late and we were exhausted so I decided to let it go until morning when I could trace the source of the problem.

During the night I had a very vivid dream. In it I saw a wall outlet with the receptacle cover off. Looking into the wall box, I could see an orange wire nut on the left hand side of the outlet. There was one wire sticking out of the wire nut, and I was told that it was the source of the problem.

When we awoke the next morning, I told Betz about the dream and then set off to the task of tracing the source of our lack of power. First, I checked the outlets in the rest of the living room. All were fine so I deduced that the problem must be on the opposite side of the wall. I tested those outlets and they worked fine as well. I began taking the covers off of every outlet I could find and, lo and behold, in the kitchen, on the opposite side of the room from the wall that was common to the one with the dead outlet, was an outlet box with an orange wire nut on the left side of the outlet that had one wire sticking out. I reconnected the wire and all of the outlets worked perfectly.

Had I simply remembered a loose wire that I had seen but not consciously acknowledged until I was asleep? I might have thought so had that particular outlet and the one in the living room not both tested perfectly only an hour or so before we went to bed.

Many times throughout the renovation of the property both Betz and I could feel Penny's presence. There was a definite sense of pleasure and satisfaction in the work we were doing. Even though our intention was to sell the property after we were done, we knew that Penny approved. Similarly, many times when I have done work around my mother's house, I knew that Sheldon was near. Lost items, hidden tools, just the right nut or bolt all seemed to present themselves at just the right time. I'd just smile and say, "Thanks, Pop." This time, it was, "Thanks, Penny."

Stephanie "Penny" Baker

Watching Over His Farm

One of the first encounters Betz and I experienced together was at Michael Lightweaver's "enchanted spiritual retreat center," Mountain Light Sanctuary (www.MountainLightSanctuary. com). The center is located at the foot of a mountain on the edge of the Pisgah National Forest in western NC, and offers space for group and personal retreats.

On our first night in one of the cabins, we were visited by "the old man." We had just settled into bed in the upper loft of the cabin when we both clearly heard the sounds of someone walking on the cabin deck, then the front door opening and footsteps in the lower room. Michael was the only other person on the property that weekend and he was up at the main house. I sensed that the visitor was not physical and was anything but malevolent.

The next morning, we asked Michael about the visitor. He smiled and told us about "Walter," the old farmer who used to own the property. He died many years ago but still keeps an eye on it. It usually takes several visits by a guest before they are graced by a visitation. We both felt honored to have been so welcomed.

Like Sheldon in the workshop, and Penny in her house, Walter has charged himself with the task of caretaker. I believe that they could easily pass over if they so choose, but for whatever reason, have decided to stay on for a while.

Michael has shared many photographs and video clips of various entities he has encountered and been allowed to record on the site. The purity of the energy there works as a focus to aide in the spiritual connections.

Welcome Back

In the summer of 2012, Betz and I decided to take a little road trip to Albright Grove Trail, up the side of a mountain in the Great Smoky Mountains National Park in Tennessee. After hiking about half way up the mountain we came upon a small settlers' cabin that has been kept intact for over 200 years. As I walked up to the cabin I was greeted with an overwhelming feeling of welcome. Not as in "welcome, stranger," but unmistakably "welcome back."

I took many photographs of the cabin and the half acre of cleared land around it. When I began to take photos of the interior of the cabin, however, I got more than I expected.

Settlers' cabin on the Albright Grove Trail, Tennessee

The first interior shot had several spheres of light that I attributed to the flash unit being skewed. The next few shots showed the spheres moving and combining in a way that the flash or lens flare could not possibly emulate. It appeared to be a family unit of man, woman, and children which moved across the room while the camera remained stationary.

A cluster of orbs moving through the cabin.

Behind the cabin, Betz discovered four sentinel trees surrounding a small spring coming out of the rocks. The energy was magnificent. We stayed there for quite a while before finishing our hike to the grove.

A Memorial

Sometimes only part of a building, a remnant, is all that is left behind to mark where someone has been. On a visit to Monticello, the Jefferson estate near Charlottesville, VA, I came across a lone standing fireplace and chimney. The cabin was gone and even the outline of the floor could no longer be clearly determined without expert guidance. It was the cabin of one of Jefferson's servants. Although technically slaves, his servants were very well treated and many felt more like hired workers.

Remains of a servant's cabin, Monticello, VA.

That was the feeling I got when I stood by the stones. It was still warm and inviting. The man who lived and worked in this cabin had a strong sense of identity and pride in his craftsmanship. He worked in leather and did fine fitting and tooling. In much the same way that a large marble obelisk stands over the grave of Thomas Jefferson in the family graveyard on the estate, this chimney marks the life of a proud man.

McCanless House

While driving around investigating the sites for the Salisbury book, I noticed a particularly remarkable house built entirely of quarried stone. Karen identified it as the Napoleon Bonaparte McCanless House and, although it was not on Karen's list, it so intrigued me that I had to stop to photograph it. She told me the story about how one of the young sons of the family had either fallen or been pushed out of a third floor window and died.

When I enlarged the photograph, my wife's elder daughter noticed an image in a ground floor window that resembles a mother cradling an infant in her arms.

The McCanless House, Salisbury, NC, with a
glowing window pane under the porch roof.

Detail of McCanless House window.

It is interesting to note that all of the first floor windows are shaded by the porch roof, yet only the top half of this particular window is illuminated. At the time that this photograph was taken, the house was for sale and unoccupied.

Chapter 7

Fully Passed and Free to Move Over and Back

To Protect Us

In 1994 I joined 19 other people, including the captain and cook, aboard a 65-foot ketch sailboat for a two-week trek through the islands of the northern Caribbean. I have sailed small boats up to about 16 feet in the past, and while the basic concepts are the same, the prospect of sailing a boat this size in open water was an exciting opportunity for me. We set out from South Beach, Miami, FL heading off to our first destination, a small coral island called Cat Cay. After a long day of snorkeling and diving on the reef, with all of the incredible plants, fish, and, yes, sharks, we headed off to Bimini Island in the Bahamas.

It was going to be a long sail and we wanted to have as much time as possible on the island, so we decided to sail straight through the night taking one hour shifts at the wheel, directly through the Bermuda Triangle.

As luck would have it, I drew the midnight watch. The boat handled like a dream. The flat bottom, designed to draw only 16" in order for the boat to navigate the shallow water over the reefs, glided effortlessly across the sea. The wheel was mounted on the open deck with a swivel chair behind it and a compass in front of it. I started out my shift sailing by the stars. A few clouds began to obscure my view so I switched to the compass, set a heading, and proceeded on. All of a sudden the bow of the boat went vertical. A rogue wave hit us head on. The boat came down with a crash as the rest of the crew and all of our equipment and supplies were tossed around the lower cabin. Several of the other crew members rushed to the deck to help lower and secure the sails and get the engines started. We were heading directly into a squall.

I lashed a rope around my waist and tied it to a deck cleat. Without a wheel house there was no other way to insure that I would not be washed overboard. I sent the rest of the crew below deck and took my position at the wheel. For the next hour I held onto that wheel for dear life. A squall is like a tornado at sea that hits from all directions at once. Each time the wind would change direction the waves would come from somewhere else. The waves reached up to 20 feet high. All I could do was aim directly for every wave I saw and try to hit them head on. The compass was spinning wildly and I had no idea what direction we were heading. I just aimed for the waves. Without a deep keel, the boat would not only rise and fall with the waves but also side slip. If we were to have been hit broadside it would have rolled the boat and we would have been 20 more souls lost in the Bermuda Triangle.

As suddenly as it started, the storm stopped. The sea went calm. The boat and all aboard survived with only minor bumps, bruises, cuts, and scratches. I shut down the engines and dropped the anchor. Captain came on deck and asked me what I was doing. I said, "Nothing," and I meant it. All was quiet. We were all safe, and I was exhausted. I suggested we rest there until first light and then we can reassess and get under way again. Captain agreed and went to bed.

First light came about four hours after we dropped anchor. The captain was able to get his GPS system back online and calculate our position. In spite of spinning in every possible direction to fight the storm and sitting for four hours, we were less than three degrees off of our original course and 30 minutes off of our original ETA. By my quick calculations I determined that it was physically impossible, but here we were, more than three hours closer than we should be.

Bimini is legend to be the gateway to the lost city of Atlantis. Under about 15 to 20 feet of water, just off Paradise Point, on the northwest side of the island lies what appears to be a man-made road. The half mile formation consists of very large, flat, square rocks that are so closely set together that you can't get the blade of a dive knife between them. The road was first foretold in a trance prophecy by Edgar Cayce in 1939 but was not discovered until 1968, when he predicted it would be found. I cannot say with assurance that it was the actual road to Atlantis but when you dive the road the energy is unmistakable.

A few days later we anchored off of a small sand bar island for an afternoon of fun and sun. I had forgotten to account for the effects of sun and libation when I decided not to take advantage of the small skiff that was shuttling crewmates from the island and swim the 200 or so yards back to the boat. About half way there, in about 20 to 30-foot-deep water, I realized that I was exhausted. I tried to call for help but no one was close enough to hear me. I remember going under for the third time and then losing consciousness. The next thing I knew I was holding on to the ladder of the boat. Was it my guide, a guardian angel, a mermaid, or the triangle? Whichever it was, thank you.

Photograph that I took from the shore of the island
just before I started to swim to the boat.

I have lost count of the number of times in my life that I
should, by all accounts, have been killed. In 1958, when my
parents separated, my mother had taken my sisters and me
from Chicago to Syracuse by train. At some point during the
night, the engine struck something on the tracks causing a
terrible crash. The shockwave that reverberated through the
train caused all of the railcars after ours to derail and roll down
a steep embankment. To this day I can vividly remember the
sounds of the crash; the breaking glass and bending steel. I can
hear the screams and cries of the injured and shocked. I can see
the lights of the emergency crews flashing and swirling through
the darkness. Why was ours the last car standing?

In college, I had a roommate who came back to the dorm
room late one evening, totally drunk. He decided to put a hot
pot of water on to boil to make coffee and then promptly passed
out. The hotpot was on top of a small cube refrigerator at the

head of my bed where I was sleeping. The water boiled and evaporated. The pot overheated and melted through the plastic top of the fridge, setting the insulation on fire. Thick smoke filled the room and when I awoke my eyes were swollen nearly shut and my throat was so swollen I couldn't speak. I rolled out of my bed on to the floor, and, somehow dragged my roommate out of the room. I made my way back into the room and grabbed the smoldering fridge and threw it out of the window into the snow. By all rights, with the source of the fire inches above my head, I should not have woken up at all. Who woke me and why?

I have been in car crashes, near air disasters, tornadoes, hurricanes, floods, landslides, and more. Every time it happens now, I am reminded of the words of Marie telling me that it was not yet my time. I have much more to do. The guides/guardians keep an eye on us. They know when it's our time to leave, when we have accomplished what we set out to do in this life, and, unless we freely choose to end it sooner, they will do all they can to protect us.

To Comfort Us

In the spring of 2013, after months of vacillation between self-confidence and trepidation, I decided to offer my psychic abilities to the public. Rather than simply allowing sessions to occur as the occasion arose I would invite the connection at the request of the client.

That April I met with Sara. She said that she felt as if something or someone was near and wanted to find out if I could detect anything. I made it clear to her that at no time prior to the session was she to give me any information about who or what she thought it might be. During the session she was instructed not to respond to anything that I may say or do in any way. Whatever would happen would happen. There were no guarantees of any kind (mostly because I honestly had no idea if this type of session-on-demand would produce any result whatsoever) but I assured her that I would describe whatever I saw, heard, or felt as it occurred.

The session began quietly. I called upon my guide to come to me and surround me with her protective energy. I asked for connection to whoever was near. I felt the familiar cold envelop me. I felt calm and safe, and the tears began to roll down my cheeks. At that moment the bell of the church next-door rang twice. I immediately felt happiness and began to smile broadly. The entity, a female in her 80's with shoulder length silver grey hair, appeared to me and told me that she loved the sound of the bells. Then she left.

It seemed like a long while before she came back, but she did return and felt the need to show me that she had long white socks on and could stand up and dance. She danced as if she was filled with joy. Twirling around with her arms spread wide in an open meadow. There were others dancing with her and she laughed and giggled like a child as she spun. There was no music, just dancing. At first it seemed as if there were two entities, both women, traveling together but I thought I might be remembering the experience with my stepsister and projecting into this session, so I didn't mention it.

I saw the letter "A", like the point of an arrow, leading to a wooded path. The path led to the open meadow where she had been dancing. At the end of the meadow stood a small, white church.

There was a light blue aura to the vision which coalesced and manifested into a sweater that was draped over the woman's shoulders, with body of the sweater on her back and the sleeves hanging down over her chest.

Suddenly, the left front fender of a large late model car appeared. It was jet black with bright chrome trim. I knew it was a convertible although I could not see the entire car. It was cruising along a country highway.

The next thing I saw was a small tin box with a hinged cover. It was about 3" wide by 5" long by 3" deep, green enamel on the outside and black on the inside. Inside the box was a single flat key, nothing else. The box was on a book shelf just above and to the right of an antique wooden writing desk. The desktop was flat, about 3' by 5'. It had three small drawers in front on either side of the open center where the chair sat, spindle legs and fine molding trim. On the top of the desk sat a lamp with a frosted glass globe. I was told that Sarah needed to find the metal box and key, but not why.

She made a point of telling me that she had been ready to die and that the "time was right." There was no fear or pain in her passing.

After the session, Sara and I discussed what I had seen and described. Her mother had died not too long ago. She was in her 80's and had silver grey hair but always wore it up on her head. Sara also had an aunt who also died in her 80s and whose hair was down at her shoulders. Her mother was bed ridden at the end of her life and had told Sara that it "was her time."

In the bed her feet would get cold and she wanted socks on to keep warm. She kept her favorite blue sweater over her shoulders in case she might get cold but rarely ever actually put it on. Her mother loved the sound of church bells and they would always make her smile. She loved to "dance," which consisted of twirling around the room with her arms outstretched.

Sara's mother and father were married in a small church in a meadow off of the Appalachian Trail. Sara's grandfather, who performed the ceremony, was a preacher who traveled along the trail on horseback, from town to town, to hold services. The symbol for the trail is composed of the letters "A" and "T" forming the shape of an arrow pointing upward, just as I had seen.

The black convertible belonged to Sara's aunt and uncle who would take it out to cruise the Blue Ridge Parkway on the weekends. The desk, the lamp, and the room that I had described was in her aunt's house. Sara did not recall ever seeing the metal box but said that she would be looking for it.

I had no expectations going into this session. Anything or nothing might happen. If I picked up anything it might have no connection to Sara at all. Each of the visions that I received seemed like non sequiturs. What possible connection could a black convertible have with church on the Appalachian Trail?

I believe that this reading was every bit as much for me as it was for Sara. There was a need for closure on her part. For her it was the reassuring confirmation that her mother and aunt were still nearby when she felt like connecting. For me it was the reassuring confirmation that what I do is a real and necessary service that I am called to offer. I have come to realize, also, that when someone comes to me and asks for a reading, it doesn't matter if I perceive a need for them or not. The fact that they were led to me is confirmation enough of their need.

Although I am still, to this day, amazed by these experiences, I was more than just a little apprehensive at the prospect of going public with my services. I went ahead and printed up business cards and I was officially "out of the closet" (so to speak).

To Reassure Us

Sometimes we may not immediately recognize the messages being delivered. We did a reading for a young lady from Florida and during that session I clearly saw a white two tiered birthday cake with blue edging around the top of each layer. The number 13 appeared as if it were the big number candles used on birthday cakes. I then saw a desk in the corner of a room which was piled high with books. I heard someone saying, "You have to keep studying, you can't give up." There was a football on a shelf as if it were a trophy or souvenir. It was signed by someone whose name I could not make out.

When I asked the young lady about what I had related she didn't see any connection or relevance to her life. I asked if she had a white cake for her 13th birthday and she couldn't remember anything like that. She had mentioned to Betz that she was in the area with a friend for her birthday and we gave discounted rate for the session as a birthday present. I asked her when her birthday had been and she said that it was actually coming up within the next week. "What day?" I asked. "Oh, on Wednesday, the 13th." (OhhhhKay!)

As we talked she told us about her brother who had passed. He loved football and collected lots of memorabilia. (Uh-huh!) Their mother would constantly press them to stick to the books and finish school. Her brother had come through to say that he was watching over her and to wish her a happy birthday.

To Give Us Guidance

In December of 1977 several friends and I were celebrating the end of the semester classes and term finals as we often did at a local pub. Tony Marren, a fraternity brother of mine, was having a particularly hard time. Totally out of character for him, his grades had suffered significantly and he was facing being dropped from the college. He didn't know how he would face his siblings, or worse, his mother, with such a disgrace.

As we sat in the bar I was greeted by the image of an older gentleman sitting in a large chair, on a large oval rug in a living room, facing a fireplace. He was very calm and comforting. I would later find out that the man was Tony's deceased father. He wanted me to reassure Tony that he would indeed finish multiple college programs, albeit not at this school. He said that Tony would travel. He would spend time in the desert and in the mountains. He would travel to a distant country, but one where the language would not be an issue. And, finally, that Tony would be "known to many."

Years later, when Tony heard that I was writing this book, he contacted me to relate how what he called "the prophecy" had come to pass. Tony had been raised devout Catholic. After leaving the college, he found great comfort in the Church of Jesus Christ of Latter Day Saints, The Mormons. He moved to Utah and lived in the mountains and desert of the Provo area.

He was sent by the Church to do missionary service in London from 1982 to 1984. Upon his return to the US he reentered college receiving an Associate's degree in Social

Sciences from Utah Valley University, a Bachelor's degree in Speech Rhetoric from Brigham Young University, and a Masters in Organizational Management from the University of Phoenix. In 2008 he founded "Operation Just One Can" advocacy effort and in 2011 was acknowledged as a World Peace Builder by the United Nations World Peace Day broadcast program. He was dubbed an Agent of Change by the Christian Science Monitor and nominated for a Nobel Peace Prize in 2012.

Was it a "prophecy of things to come" or a "self-fulfilling prophecy" that he applied in order to change the course of his life? I believe that it is the recognition of the message that rekindles the purpose we set for ourselves in this lifetime. Not charting a new course so much as getting back on the course we had forgotten or disregarded.

I don't consider myself a "prophet." The prophets of the Old Testament did not divine answers from within themselves. They related the predictions and warnings that were given to them by God or the Angels. Did Edgar Cayce travel, perhaps through astral-projection, in order to experience his visions firsthand or was he told by some other being or entity? Either way, he had to get the information before he could relate it. Likewise, I simply relay the messages that are delivered to me. If I exhibit pre-cognitive abilities it is because the guides, who are not bound by time or space, have given me the information. They tell me what I or the clients need to know in order to continue on our paths. In this case, Tony was consumed with self-doubt and disappointment. Perhaps, he simply needed to be given reassurance and a nudge in the right direction.

To Give Us Closure

My closest friend in college, Walter Cook, and I started out together as freshmen in Political Science. Though I would later change my major to Art and Photography, we stayed very close throughout college and still to this day.

In the spring of our junior year, Walt had been feeling exceptionally sad and lonely. It was obviously more than upper-classman anxiety and stress. One evening, while standing out on the front porch of our fraternity house, he confided in me that he felt like something or someone was following him. Almost instantly, I felt the presence of a spirit. My guide rushed in and the contact was made. I told Walt that I sensed his father with us. Even though we were close, I did not know that Walt's father, a Navy pilot, had died when Walter was just a boy. He never talked about it to anyone.

With that I was transported, not only in time and space but in body. I was the pilot of a jet fighter aircraft. I was flying in toward a shoreline. I could see it just about a mile ahead. There were two other jet fighters, one on either side of my wings. I could see the other pilots through the cowls of the planes. Suddenly, there was an explosion at the tail of my plane. I clutched a medal that hung around my neck as the flames rushed forward and my plane went down into the sea. The medal was comprised of four ovals over a center circle that formed a cross or cruciform. The ovals of the medal, referred to as the "Catholic Four-Way," depict the Sacred Heart of Jesus, the "Miraculous Medal" image of Mary, St. Joseph, and St. Christopher. On the flat reverse side of this medal I could read two dates, MM/DD/YYYY, engraved one above the other.

Next I was in my rack (Navy for bunk bed) on an aircraft carrier out at sea. I was writing a letter. It was four pages long on rice paper. I read the letter aloud, word for word. It told of my recent experiences and my plans to be home for the coming holidays. There was great joy and excitement in the letter with the anticipation of being with my family again.

The next thing I knew; I was standing at the door of an apartment in my full dress uniform. A woman, whom I presumed to be my wife, was there with our young son. She was wearing a knee length yellow dress with white polka dots and she informed me that she was pregnant with our daughter.

With that, it was over. It seemed like a matter of a few minutes but was, in fact, over an hour. Walter confirmed all of the events and details I had described and said that they were in reverse chronological order from his father's death to his happiest memories. Walt's mother had received the letter I had read just days before he was reported shot down. The wing pilots had reported that the missile had hit the tail section of the jet and that the blast rushed forward engulfing the plane. Walt's father wore a medal around his neck that had the birthdates of Walt and his sister engraved on the back side.

Some would describe my experience as "channeling." Having experienced both mediumship and channeling, I can attest that the two are not the same. Channeling allows an entity to enter the reader's body and assume the use of their voice and sometimes physical abilities. The medium connects with the entity to observe and share their experiences and listen to their messages and then relate those messages to the client.

To Say Goodbye

It had been about three years since a dear friend of ours, Rose, had lost her husband, Chris. We had stopped by her small apartment to visit when I felt the unmistakable presence of someone who wanted to connect. I asked Rose if she wanted me to do a reading and she eagerly agreed.

I knew that Chris had been somewhat of a gourmet cook and he would prepare wonderfully delicious appetizers and other dishes to be served at their wine shop. That was why I was confused when the first image I received was a bowl of macaroni and cheese with ground beef and chopped tomatoes. Rose revealed that it had been Chris' favorite comfort food. He had just said, "Hello."

I saw a keychain with a flat brass house key. Also on the chain was a metal charm, a bit larger than a quarter. The charm was greenish in color and heart shaped. I told Rose that it looked like a guitar pick. That was when she broke into tears. She stood up and went into the bedroom returning with a key ring. On the ring was a small leather pouch which contained Chris' guitar picks. He confirmed that it was, indeed him.

Finally, I saw a dark leather jacket hanging on a peg, but not in a closet. He told me that it was time to put it away. Rose confessed that Chris' jacket was still hanging on the coat rack by the front door. She couldn't bring herself to put it away. He was telling her that it was time to let him go and begin to move on with her own life.

Chapter 8

Good vs. Evil

Are There Evil Spirits?

There are, and always will be, those whose intentions are not for the good of the universe, but rather for the perceived good or gain for the self. (So, Mr. Spock, exactly when does the needs of the one outweigh the needs of the many?) For some this gain is pursued with disregard, conscious or otherwise, for the effect that it may have on those around them. John Calvin claimed that these individuals were preselected by God to be evil. If that were the case, we would come into this life without the capacity to choose to be good as well. There would be no such thing as true unconditional love because it would have been predestined and not given freely. Predestination negates the possibility to learn and grow. Contrary to Calvin, we have the free will to choose whether to change or never move on from that state.

Can evil be destroyed? Newtonian physicists will tell you that energy can neither be created nor destroyed, only transferred or changed. Quantum physicists will tell you that matter in its most fundamental level can be created from nothing and returned to nothing. All we can hope for is to protect ourselves from that negative energy and maintain enough of a balance so that we can progress and ultimately learn more of the answers that presently elude us.

Questions that I am often asked, however, are not about the balance of nature, but rather about the existence of evil or demonic entities. "Are there devils and demons who are out to destroy us?" Hebrew tradition identifies earthbound spirits as the Dybbuk, or clinging spirit. The evil Dybbuk are divided into two groups: those who enter the body of a living person and direct that person's conduct; and, those who have suffered a "karet," meaning that they have been cut off from God because of evil deeds during their life. Good spirits include the Ibbur, or spirits of a righteous ancestors, and the Maggid, or the spirit guides. In the Old Testament, Isaiah and Ezekiel both speak of an angel who challenged the authority of God. Because of his impertinence, he was cast out of Heaven and given the title of "Satan." Interestingly, the word "satan" in Hebrew and Arabic languages does not mean "evil." Rather, it translates to "adversary."

Earlier I described the vision of the other side that Marie revealed to me. Along that journey much more was given to me. She provided answers to many of the questions I had long held about life and afterlife.

When the body dies, the energy that is within each of us hopefully moves on to another plane. We may call that place Heaven, Valhalla, Olympus, or whatever we choose. It is the collective energy of all of us. It is neither place nor time yet it is everywhere and always.

While we will not be likely to meet an old man with a long white beard sitting on a throne with a record book of all of our earthly deeds (no, not Santa Claus), we will be given the opportunity to reflect on our past life. Each life brings with it lessons to be learned and previous errors to correct. This is sometimes referred to as Karma. What we must decide is whether we learned the lessons we came here to learn or not.

In many ways, our lives and the afterlife are like school. We start out as toddlers in preschool and kindergarten, and with the completion of the lessons of each level we progress toward our doctorates. When Jesus came to the life reported in the New Testament of the Christian Bible he was already way ahead of the majority of us. While he was in graduate school the rest of us were fighting over the sandbox in primary school. Many of us still are. He brought with him knowledge and skills that made him god-like to the people of that time. Healing, astral projection, telepathy, clairvoyance, precognition, telekinesis, levitation, and even resurrection were all abilities that were reserved only for the gods or demons.

It is interesting to note that nowhere in the Bible does Jesus refer to himself as God or the ultimate perfection. Over and over, he calls himself the Son of God. "Thy will be done," (Matthew 6:10). "For I have come down from heaven, not to do my own will, but the will of Him who sent me," (John 6:38). "Father, if Thou art willing, remove this cup from me; nevertheless, not my will, but Thine be done," (Luke 22:42). There are many, many more.

There is only one line in which Jesus says, "I and the Father are one," (John 10:30). The original Aramaic (later translated into Greek, and then Latin, and then to English) word for "one" that was used in the text literally translates to one in purpose, however, not one in being. He also said, "The way to the Father is through me," (John 14:6). How can we reach the ultimate level of perfection if we do not first attain his level?

As we move up through the levels, we grow and learn and mature. Think about a toddler who wants a toy or candy in the store. Mom says no and the toddler throws a tantrum. As the child matures toward adulthood, it becomes easier to reason with them and to explain why certain decisions are made. When maturation is hindered or stunted, for any number of reasons, so is the ability to connect actions with consequences. Society calls these "bad" decisions. In much the same way, young or immature souls may behave inappropriately, and societies and religions label them as "evil." Therefore, I return to my earlier question of, "Are there devils and demons who are out to destroy us?"

The more psychic experiences I have and the deeper I delve into the spiritual nature of these experiences, the less I believe in devils. Rather, I have come to accept these entities as those who have not yet achieved a higher level of understanding of the consequences of their actions. They are more like children and they require us to act more like adults when we confront them. My stepfather had a saying that, if you want to be good at hunting squirrels, you have to be just a little smarter than the squirrel. Likewise, no one ever bagged a squirrel by arguing with it. When we are confronted by forces that we perceive as evil, it is on us to stand firm and not give into the tantrum.

Uninvited

Sometimes things can happen without our will or intention. I had been experiencing what I had initially thought were bad dreams. It was like I was fully conscious and awake but still asleep at the same time. I couldn't move from the bed. I couldn't speak to cry for help. All I could do was to stagger my breathing so violently that it would alert my roommate and he would shake me out of the state. Sleep experts refer to this state as "waking dreams" or "sleep paralysis." This is a normal occurrence for many people and usually lasts only a few seconds as the body is working to slowly bring us out of dream sleep to consciousness without thrashing and physically hurting ourselves. When the state lasts for several minutes or longer it can be terrifying. The body is still in paralysis but the brain is now fully aware.

As these waking dreams were becoming more frequent I could also sense several entities in the room with me. They were hovering as if waiting for an opportunity to move in. I had been taking classes in parapsychology with Dr. Timothy DeChenne, Ph.D., Professor of Psychology and Paranormal Studies at the State University of New York at Geneseo, and went to ask him about these events. He agreed that the extended states were abnormal and arranged to run some tests. First he tested me for susceptibility to suggestion (hypnosis). During my classes on Parapsychology I had the opportunity to work with a bio-feedback machine that measures brainwave activity at various states of consciousness. With practice I was able to achieve delta mind state while fully conscious. After several other tests and exercises he determined that I could accept suggestions but still exercise my will if I felt threatened or taken advantage of. He recorded the session on a reel to reel tape recorder (state of the art at the time).

The doctor made sure that I was comfortable. He put me under a light hypnosis to relax me and allow him to also have control over whatever might happen. The first question he asked was, "Is the entity here?" I mentally felt around the room and detected something to my left and slightly behind me. I told him that it was in the room. He asked if I would agree to let it in as long as he was able to stop the session at any time. As soon as I agreed I felt four separate entities encircle me. One was pulling at my feet from under the chair I was sitting in. One was at my left side pulling the skin at my waist. A third was pulling my hands around my left side. The fourth was stretching my face toward the back of my head.

It was easy to see the indentations of fingers grabbing and pulling at my hands. My face was drawn up into a grotesque smile. Again the doctor asked if it was here. All four entities, in distinct voices in unison, answered through me, *"We are here. We **are** here. We are **here**."* With each repeat they would emphasize a different word. He asked them, "What do you want?" *"We want **him**,"* came the reply. "Why do you want him?" *"Because he's open."* "When will you let him go?" *"When he dies."* "Where are you from?" *"We're from **HELL**."* At that point the doctor ended the session.

Demonomancy, the summoning of demons, was not our intention. When we played back the tape all four voices were clearly audible. The tape ran far longer than the few minutes that I thought I had experienced. The finger marks from their grasps were visible for almost an hour afterward. The doctor said that it was the first time that he was truly terrified of a session. He left me with a subconscious suggestion to block anything from coming in.

It had not occurred to me at the time that I had not sensed my guide anywhere in the room. I had to learn to always be aware of what is around me, to encase myself in the white light, and to make sure that my guide was there at all times to protect me. I also had to learn that I am the one who is in charge. These were not demons, as we have come to expect, but rather pranksters playing the "I can scare you" game. I won't let adolescent souls bully me. It is critical that we are in control of what we allow in, when we allow it in, and what we block out.

Protect Yourself

It is my assumption that if you have read this far you are more than a little curious about the psychic realm and are at least dabbling in what some refer to as the "occult." The most important advice I could give you right now is BE CAREFUL!

As noted earlier, there are those immature souls who will act out inappropriately or even violently when they don't get their way. Sometimes they will play "games" with us just for fun or spite. It is essential that we recognize them and deal with them accordingly.

I have confronted so-called malevolent entities. Early on, had I attempted this alone the results could have been disastrous. Over the years I have learned many methods of raising my awareness and protecting myself. Every successful psychic and/ or medium I have met practices some method of centering and protection before they begin a reading.

Those who use focal points or divination tools such as Tarot cards, crystal balls, Ouija Boards, or talismans learn that it is extremely important to cleanse the energy of these objects before they begin. It is just as easy for "evil" to communicate through them as it is for good. I cringe when I hear about children playing with an Ouija Board without guidance. Would you give a child a loaded handgun and then walk away?

I have read many methods of cleansing divination tools, and a few techniques tend to be constant. First and most important is clearly stating your intention. You need to hold yourself, your tools, and all around you in a positive light.

At the start of my sessions my wife, Betz, will lead everyone in a short meditation for centering, grounding, protection, and focus. This brings everyone involved into the light and energy of my guides and all who surround them. Take your time with the meditation and bring your full consciousness to the method.

- Begin by sitting comfortably, back straight, both feet on the floor.

- Take a deep, cleansing breath, inhaling slowly through the nose – then exhale slowly through the mouth, releasing the day and any cares or concerns.

- Take in another deep, cleansing breath, and again exhale, consciously allowing your physical body to relax.

- Imagine a beam of radiant white light emanating from the heart of the Divine – envision it entering the top of your head.

- See and feel this light descend, and imagine it centering itself in your heart. Allow the light to warm and expand the energy of your heart, enlivening your compassion, your empathy, your love while simultaneously sheltering the core of your beingness.

- Imagine the brilliant white light filling your entire chest cavity ... continuing to expand into your torso ... flowing down and through your legs and arms.

- This immaculate white light continues to expand until it fully envelopes your entire body. It surrounds you. Envelopes and enfolds you. Shelters and protects you.

- Trust with complete knowing that any and all information you receive must first come through this Divine white light.

- Trust that any and all information received will be of the highest and best good of all concerned.

- Trust that this light is with you, surrounds you, and fills you at all times and in all circumstances.
- You need only set the intention… And remember.

(Visit Betz' website, www.BetzMckeown.com, for more information on Spirituality Coaching and Energy Healing.)

Many people will begin with a prayer. Our friend, Donna Spring Gulick, offers excellent prayers for clearing.

> "I ask that this area be cleared and cleansed. That all energies that are less than helpful be sealed in their own light and returned to the Source for purification. I ask that this room and all within it be surrounded by and filled with the White [Christ] Light."

Or simply,

> "I will only receive those energies which are for my highest good and the highest good of all concerned."

She says, "I don't think of it as being a protection, as much as a spam filter and a focus of my intention to serve this person in the highest and best way...My words aren't identical every time, but the following themes are ALWAYS in the prayer."

> "Allness" of God, thank you for the Love, Wisdom, Power and Light in _____, in me and in all. Thank you for our many blessings - known or unknown to us. Thank you for the

Guidance, Protection and Assistance we receive. We now open to the Guides and Angels who work with _____ and those who work with me, for his/her Highest Good and the Highest Good of all concerned. We open to healing, information, transformation and leaps in consciousness through the Christ Light, in its inclusiveness of all Truth and all Love. Filled with and surrounded by Divine Light, we give thanks and we listen. Amen.

(Visit www.DonnaSpringGulick.com for more techniques on centering, clearing, and releasing)

It is not so much the specific words or phrases, or even the entities or deities we pray to, as it is the intention we project when we meditate or pray. Believe it, affirm it, and truly feel it. The act of praying or meditating sets the energy. I recommend that you do this daily, before and after every session.

Another common method for cleansing is smudging. Everything - plants, animals, humans, minerals and even the Earth - has an aura or energy field. The energy can be positive or negative. Smudging clears the negative energies and allows the positive energies to grow. Cleanse your divination tools, your location, and yourself. The technique is not difficult. There are many books on the subject or you can go on the internet and find numerous sites that will direct you through the process. The important thing, again, is to be firm in your intentions. Hold the light and love throughout the ceremony and know that you are in control. Call on your guide and the positive entities as you displace the negative.

When I first learned the importance of protection I would envision myself surrounded by a sphere of light. I could see, feel, hear, smell, taste, and experience the light. I would look ahead and to the right and see a door. I'd open the door and command that anyone who wished to contact me must come through the door. The first one through was my guide and she would make sure that only the right spirits would follow. Now, I recognize my circle of 15 and they direct those who desire or need contact into the circle.

Once you have found the cleansing and protecting practices that work for you (and you will know by the energy you feel), practice your techniques often and become accustomed to the presence of your guides. As you learn and develop, you will find that their energy is your energy. Their circle is your sphere of protection. Don't become complacent. I remind myself of the sphere and my connection to my guides on a daily basis.

Exorcism or Understanding?

What do we do when we are called on to confront those adolescent spirits who throw tantrums and cause trouble? I received a very distressed call from a woman who claimed that something was terribly wrong at her house. Her teenaged son had become isolated and argumentative and she felt like a thick wall of energy was trying to keep her from the upper floor of the house where his bedroom was. Light bulbs were blowing out throughout the house. Television channels were changing on their own. She feared that he may have been dabbling with the occult and unleashed an evil entity on their home.

We began the session at her house with a moment of centering and clearly stating our intentions. I called my guides to surround us all and keep us in their light. Our goal was to connect with whatever was there, find out its purpose, and, if need be, send it on.

I entered the house and felt the energy draw me toward the stairs where I encountered the "wall." The entity told me, in no uncertain terms, that I was not welcome. I pushed through what felt like a thick cloud of energy and up the stairs in spite of the entity. I intended to confront it head on. Moving from room to room to locate the source, I returned to the hallway where it then said to me, "If you're not leaving, then sit your butt down here and I'll tell you what's going on." I sat on the floor and it proceeded to explain itself in no uncertain terms. The entity was female and older. I got the sense of a grandmother or older aunt. She was very upset with what was going on between the homeowner and her son. She repeated, several times, "This fighting has to stop!"

She had followed the family from a previous residence but that was not her home. She had taken on the task of "protecting" the son from what she perceived as his mother's hardline restrictions. "He needs his space. He needs to be allowed to grow up." Her energy was feeding off of the son's teenage rebellion and had amplified the tension and stress.

At that point I realized that there was no evil entity here. There was confusion, misunderstanding, and anger. I needed to try to set things straight. I told the homeowner that she needed to ease back on her reins a bit. The son was told that he needed to accept the fact that it was still his mother's house and she was fully entitled to set the house rules. I told the grandmother that she had to accept those rules as well.

The energy in the house began to shift almost immediately. I recently spoke with the homeowner and she still feels the energy of the grandmother upstairs but knows that it won't prevent her from going up there. There is still the teenage rebellion but it is far less confrontational. And grandma hasn't blown another light bulb since.

Closing the Session

Following any sessions, it is always a good practice to end with stated intentions of closure and thankfulness. Return to the here and now, and make sure to bring all who are with you to a place of peace and calm. Release the energies that you and all who are with you brought together at the beginning of the session.

When I am in contact with an entity who is related to the client either as family or close friend, they typically open the session by relating personal details that identify them to the client. Likewise, at the end of the session, they will often close with a specific memory or anecdote that lets the client know that all is well or that the necessary message has been delivered. At this point the session is pretty much over and the participants' comments and reactions will have no effect on what has been communicated. Now I can consciously address the participants in the room. I share the emotional and physical feelings that I experienced, which may or may not have been expressed during the reading. It's interesting to note, as I have illustrated in several earlier accounts, that sometimes the participants don't immediately recognize the significance of the symbolic or metaphoric messages delivered until we put the pieces together in the follow-up discussions (and sometimes not until much later). This is one reason that I record my sessions whenever possible and send the participants an unedited copy along with any residual messages I may have received within a few days of the session.

I was doing a Skype reading for a client in North Carolina, and at the end of the session the entity made it a point to tell her not to forget the bunch of carrots. I clearly saw a large bunch of carrots with greens still intact, tied in a neat bundle, lying on top of a butcher block counter in the middle of her kitchen. The client insisted that she did not even like carrots and could not understand why I would refer to them. The entity again, and this time more adamantly repeated, "Don't forget the carrots!" I just told her to take it at face value and leave it at that. Two weeks later she called to say that she was cleaning out her refrigerator when she found a bunch of carrots she had bought for juicing and completely forgotten about. Message delivered.

After the feedback portion of the session is finished to everyone's satisfaction, it is time to fully close the connection. Don't carry the energy or the entities home with you. If there is a need to follow up, you can select the time and place for the next reading. For now, release and return.

Be sure to thank the guides, angels, spirits, and all entities who helped you with the session. Ending with a prayer of blessing and gratitude is a good way to state your intention of closure and keep the energies open for future connections. It can be as simple as "Thank you." I can't say it often enough - it's your intention that drives the outcome.

Chapter 9

Discovery

More Than One Guide

In 2012, Betz and I stopped into a gift shop in Asheville, NC which offered a variety of items from around the world. It was here that we met Lewisa. She is a psychic reader and we had a couple's reading done by her. Lewisa immediately recognized me as one who is connected with the spirit side. The bond between Lewisa and me formed that day will continue throughout this lifetime. I'm sure that it had been forged many lifetimes ago.

During the two-and-a-half-hour drive back to our home, I received several messages from my guide. One of those was that I needed to write this book.

2013 was a year of unfolding. The most profound revelation was that my guide is not alone in facilitating my connections. She is one of 15 entities. She introduced me to the Circle of 15 during a particularly deep and clear meditation. Each entity has its own identity and purpose. Together, they open the complete path. When I enter my deep meditative state I see the group standing around me, encased in a sphere of pure light, ready to offer the guidance I need to help heal the person who has come to me for help.

I was intrigued by the number 15. In doing research on that number in religious/spiritual references, I found it quite interesting, if not coincidental, that the number 15 also happens to be the number of Archangels identified by name and purpose in the early Judeo-Christian texts. Doreen Virtue, in her book, *Archangels 101,* offers a concise reference guide to these 15 archangels including their identity, origin, purpose, auric color, and other distinguishing features. Her many books on the topic are available through www.hayhouse.com.

The Heavenly Host comprises a multitude of levels of angelic hierarchy; these are not, by any means, the only archangels. Religious texts refer to legions. Virtue's list of the primary archangels in order of dominance are:

1. Michael, the protector. "He who is like God"
2. Raphael, the healer. "God heals"
3. Gabriel, the messenger. "The strength of God"
4. Uriel, understanding. "The light of God"
5. Chamuel, universal peace. "He who sees God"
6. Ariel, nature. "The lion (lioness) of God"
7. Metatron, sacred geometry. "Human who became an archangel"
8. Sandalphon, prayer connection. "Brother"
9. Azrael, bereavement and good death. "Whom God helps"
10. Jophiel, uplifting and clearing. "Beauty of God"
11. Haniel, awakening and trusting of spiritual abilities. "Grace of God"
12. Raziel, Secrets of the universe and past lives. "Secrets of God"
13. Raguel, healing arguments. "Friend of God"
14. Jeremiel, clairvoyance. "Mercy of God"
15. Zadkiel, facts and figures. "Righteousness of God"

I also found it beautifully reassuring that she did not identify any of them as being God's hand in vengeance, punishment or destruction. They work individually or together in any number of combinations to guide and assist us as needed.

Coincidentally, the New Testament of the Christian Bible names 15 apostles. While only 11 or 12 are together at any given time, three more are identified due to substitutions, such as in the case of Judas Iscariot. Between the Books of Mark and Matthew the 15 identified Apostles include:

1. Andrew
2. Bartholomew
3. James, son of Alpheus
4. James, son of Zebedee
5. John, son of Zebedee
6. Judas Iscariot
7. Judas, son of James
8. Lebbaeus
9. Matthew
10. Nathanael
11. Phillip
12. Simon
13. Simon Peter
14. Thaddaeus
15. Thomas

While scholars may argue whether some of these names may or may not be different names for the same person, there is no doubt that 15 different names are cited. Each of the Apostles had different strengths and virtues to offer to the ministry of Jesus and to carrying on his teachings after his death.

Biblical references to the number 15 are numerous. Many Jewish holidays occur on the 15ᵗʰ of the month and the number is represented on their calendars as 9 and 6 (teth, vav) rather than the traditional 10 and 5 (yodh, heh) because the later also spells one of the Jewish names for God.

Isaiah 38:2, 4-5 states, "Hezekiah turned his face to the wall and prayed to the Lord. Then the word of the Lord came to Isaiah: 'Go and tell Hezekiah, this is what the Lord, the God of your father David, says: I have heard your prayer and seen your tears: I will add fifteen years to your life.'"

The King James Version of the Bible, Deuteronomy 5:4-20, lists the 15 Commandments given by God to Moses, not 10.

1. I am the LORD thy God, which brought thee out of the land of Egypt, from the house of bondage.
2. Thou shalt have none other gods before me.
3. Thou shalt not make thee any graven image, or any likeness of anything that is in heaven above, or that is in the earth beneath, or that is in the waters beneath the earth:
4. Thou shalt not bow down thyself unto them, nor serve them: for I the LORD thy God am a jealous God, visiting the iniquity of the fathers upon the children unto the third and fourth generation of them that hate me,
5. And shewing mercy unto thousands of them that love me and keep my commandments.

6. Thou shalt not take the name of the LORD thy God in vain: for the LORD will not hold him guiltless that taketh his name in vain.

7. Keep the Sabbath day to sanctify it, as the LORD thy God hath commanded thee.

8. Six days thou shalt labour, and do all thy work:

9. But the seventh day is the Sabbath of the LORD thy God: in it thou shalt not do any work, thou, nor thy son, nor thy daughter, nor thy manservant, nor thy maidservant, nor thine ox, nor thine ass, nor any of thy cattle, nor thy stranger that is within thy gates; that thy manservant and thy maidservant may rest as well as thou.

10. And remember that thou wast a servant in the land of Egypt, and that the LORD thy God brought thee out thence through a mighty hand and by a stretched out arm: therefore, the LORD thy God commanded thee to keep the Sabbath day.

11. Honour thy father and thy mother, as the LORD thy God hath commanded thee; that thy days may be prolonged, and that it may go well with thee, in the land which the LORD thy God giveth thee.

12. Thou shalt not kill.

13. Neither shalt thou commit adultery.

14. Neither shalt thou steal.

15. Neither shalt thou bear false witness against thy neighbour.

The Exodus 20:1-17 version has somewhat different wording and adds "thou shalt not covet thy neighbour's house; thou shalt not covet thy neighbour's wife, nor his maidservant, nor his ox, nor his ass, nor any thing that is thy neighbour's." These have been conveniently consolidated down to the ten that Christians of various denominations so vehemently argue over to this day.

Scientifically, 15 is the atomic number of phosphorus, an essential mineral that is required by every cell in the body for normal function. When phosphorus is exposed to the air, however, it spontaneously bursts into a brilliant flame.

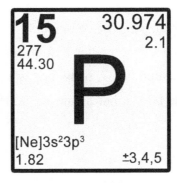

Mathematically, it is interesting to note that fifteen is a triangular number. Note the arrangement of balls on a pool table; 1 ball, then 2, then 3, then 4, then 5 forming a perfect triangle.

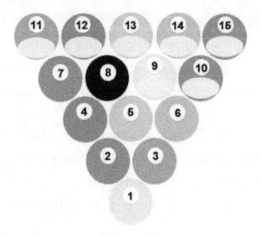

In the binary language of computers, 15 is what is called a "repdigit" which the computer recognizes as 1111. Fifteen is also a pentatope number. A pentatope is a geometric figure that most humans have a hard time visualizing because it is a 5-celled, four-dimensional object that does not exist as a 3-dimensional form.

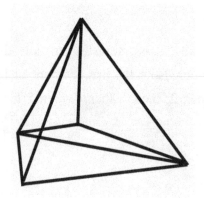

The Chinese legend of "Lo Shu," from sometime around 2700 B.C.E., tells about a great flooding of the Lo River that destroyed the villages and farm fields. The villagers tried to appease the river god by offering a sacrifice whenever the river flooded. A turtle would appear from the river and walk around the sacrifice. One day a child noticed a pattern on the turtle's shell. There were dots representing numbers that were arranged in a 3-by-3 grid pattern. The numbers in each column, row, and diagonal equaled the same sum: fifteen. This is called the magic square or Lo Shu and is used to this day as a tool in Feng-Shui.

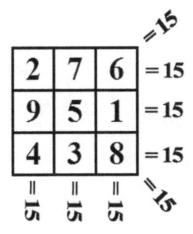

Fifteen became the number of sacrifices needed in order to make the river god happy. The First Chinese calendar, created during that same time period, was based on a solar formula that was woven into the lunar cycles and then divided equally into 24 node points, or Chieh-ch'i, separated by a span of 15 days each.

In numerology, the number 15 reduces to 6 (1+5), which is a number of "great love and harmony." Unfortunately, the number 15 (The Ides of March) wasn't quite so lucky for Julius Caesar.

Universal Knowledge

In 2014, I was attending a Unity service in Winston-Salem, NC. Suddenly, I saw the 15 guides in a wide circle hovering just above the congregation. This time, however, they were not glowing in the darkness. They were radiating in the light. In the light I could see they were not alone. They were surrounded by millions upon millions of souls, all sharing in and contributing to the light. This time, my eyes were wide open.

I realized that my role as the psychic and medium has been a lesson on my path toward greater awareness. A medium is merely a messenger, a data technician, who can access that universal web of information; one who can "Google in a topic and get some answers."

Courtroom lawyers learn early in their training that it can be a very effective technique in persuading a jury to occasionally and carefully make a point that you know will be objected to and removed from the record. What cannot be removed, however, is the fact that the jurors heard it. "You can't un-ring a bell."

On the astral plane, we can access the total sum of knowledge we have acquired throughout our lifetimes. We can then choose to acquire more knowledge or remain static with what we have. At that time, we will decide what knowledge to consciously carry with us into the next life.

If we can choose to acquire knowledge, can we also choose to lose it? Can we "un-ring that bell?" In a computer we store information in the memory drives. We can call up any specific information as we need it and ignore the rest. When information is deleted from the hard drive of a computer it isn't really gone. Restoration software, like that which is used by law enforcement agencies, can retrieve data thought deleted years ago. Until the drive is completely reformatted, removing all data and, in the case of the main hard drive, the programming, the data is still there. You just can't see it. Can we randomly choose to totally delete knowledge or is it simply relegated to hidden files?

An intriguing theory examined by Ervin Laszlo talks about the Akashic Field ("Science and the Akashic Field: An Integral Theory of Everything"). Akasha, in the eastern traditions, is the end of time and space where all energy and matter combine and dissolve. We can tap into this field and have access to the entire universe of knowledge at will, interacting with every other organism simultaneously. Laszlo gives numerous examples of this phenomenon. From the seemingly spontaneously choreographed movements of the smallest sub-atomic particles to the apparently random and chaotic movement of the universe, all things are interconnected. Microparticles existing in the same quantum state which are not physically connected may be separated by great distances; they form what are called Einstein-Podolski-Rosen (EPR) pairs that exhibit identical and simultaneous reactions to stimulation.

Since the 1930s, anthropologists have reported stories of aboriginal tribes in Australia who appear to have the ability to communicate detailed information over vast distances without the aid of visual or audible connection. Scientists have been trying to explain this phenomenon of cognitive telepathy since as early as 1885. The American Society of Psychical Research set up studies wherein two people, a "sender" and a "receiver," were placed in separate rooms. Images, smells, or two-digit numbers were presented to the sender and the receiver would report his or her impressions.

I mentioned earlier that we are all interconnected: vast sea of individual souls, all separate, all joined. The Akashic Field doesn't melt our individuality into a single mass of Brahmanic knowledge. It connects us like a universal super-computer. It is estimated that the storage capacity of the human brain, if we had the capability of full access, could be as high as 2.5 petabytes. (One petabyte is approximately 1,000 terabytes or one million gigabytes. That's about 500 billion pages of standard printed text or 500 million floppy disks of data.) Try to imagine billions upon billions of brains working together in a network.

Therefore, do we acquire knowledge or simply access it? If we have the ability to access all of the accumulated knowledge of all time from this infinite cosmic field, then it would not be possible to unlearn anything. We just simply choose to forget. Sometimes the information that we have stored away comes back to the surface. Have you ever found yourself in a situation where you knew the answer or could perform a task that you had no previous knowledge of or training for? Parapsychologists call this phenomenon Anomalous Cognition. I believe that it is our psyche reconnecting to the Akashic Field in order to retrieve the information that we need.

For me, the idea of a cosmic central data base, ready and available for access at any time, reinforces the need for multiple lifetimes and Karmic growth. Even though we now have an international internet with access to billions upon billions of files of data on virtually every subject known to mankind, we still need schools to teach the students how and why to use the information effectively. Knowledge and technology without purpose is useless.

If we have the ability to tap into the knowledge of all time and space, why, then, are there earthbound spirits? Wouldn't they know that they can move on? It's one thing to possess knowledge. It's a different thing to possess a metacognitive understanding of what you know or are capable of. Consider the vast numbers of people who have been killed on the battlefields of wars throughout time and remain earthbound. Some are still trying to win the battle. Some don't realize or refuse to accept that they are dead. Unfortunately, one reason that young men and women are sent in to fight the battles is that they still have a strong sense of invincibility. Human ego is a powerful emotion.

Transition comes with the acceptance of the end of one state of being and the beginning of another. The doctor told my mother that, at the end, Sheldon would just drift off to sleep and not wake up. Far from it. He woke in terrible distress: the kidneys could not eliminate the toxins in his body and the emphysema had caused fluid to collect in his lungs. He was literally drowning and he was terrified. Because his condition was so deteriorated, there was nothing we could do at this point but help him pass.

I am confident that my holding him and talking to him in a calm voice helped him to let go physically and accept his death.

When I placed my hand over his face and closed his eyelids I knew that he had accepted his reconnection to the Akashic Field of knowledge and moved on to consider his next level.

Changes

The transitions that I have been experiencing during this life are truly profound. I started out with a single guide. I would close my eyes and allow her to escort me through the darkness to that place where my connections are made. I would drop into a deep trance state where I had no sense of space or time. Often I wasn't even aware of what was being said through me. Over the years, readings have come more often and more easily. The one guide expanded into the fifteen. I now clearly see them all as they form a circle of light in the darkness, with me and whomever I would be reading for in the center.

I no longer fall into a deep trance, although my perception of time is still very distorted. As my awareness of the circle of energy grew, I realized that I could call upon the individual guides to intercede for the particular needs of my clients. Each guide or angel will offer their specific ability as well as adding to the energy of the whole.

My work has expanded from impromptu readings for friends and family to readings for anyone who needs it, by appointment. I have expanded my reach from face-to-face readings to doing readings over the phone and internet. I have also taken on the challenge of group readings.

When I first began to offer readings to my clients I would ask that no words be spoken by the client until the reading was over and then open up to question and answer with the client. I still try to keep the informational input from the client that might influence my reading to a minimum, but the reads now tend to be more conversational and informal.

When I hold a session or even do an impromptu reading, I begin by closing my eyes and envisioning Marie standing in front of me. We are encased in a sphere of pure light and soon all of the other guides become clearly visible. The 15 guides form a wide circle around me. I am still facing Marie and now project an image of my client between me and Marie. We are all now in the center of the guides, surrounded by all beings, from all time, and throughout all space.

The questions and answers, the messages, greetings, and warnings all flow through me as through a telephone cable. It is essential that I relate everything that I see, hear, or sense as the session proceeds. Even the most obscure or seemingly insignificant item can often have profound relevance. It's not up to me to decide if the item is worthwhile. This was an important and difficult lesson for me to learn. I had to stop second-guessing myself and give my faith to the guides. Sometimes the messages and images I receive can seem totally detached, like a string of complete non sequiturs. Often, I will ask the guides if the images are real or my own imagination playing tricks and trying to fill in the space with random memories. Usually, the guides are pretty adamant if the message is important.

I have come to realize that my insecurity came from the fear of interjecting my own thoughts or opinions into the readings. I've learned that it doesn't matter. No matter what I'm hearing, feeling, or thinking, say it anyway. What may seem totally irrelevant to me usually holds a special significance for those around me.

The messages are not for me. They are not mine to analyze or justify. I do not attempt to parse or interpret. For those for whom the messages are intended, the meanings are or will soon become obvious.

This became even more important when I began doing group readings because there are often several messages coming through simultaneously for different people in the group. The messages tend to get mixed and cross over from one person to another. I have no idea who the messages are for. In order to try to keep everything organized, I envision the clients in different areas of the sphere of light related to their physical location in the room. I can then turn to the guides or entities in that area to deliver messages to the appropriate person. Having a team of guides helps reduce the clutter and confusion. I can move from one message to another, realizing that they are from separate beings.

I did discover an interesting problem when I attempted to do two group readings in one day. An important message for a woman in the second group was delivered during the first session. The message was very clear and detailed, and I couldn't understand why no one in the room could relate to it. At the end of the second session, a woman in that group came to me and asked specifically about her deceased father. When she described him to me it all became clear.

Fortunately, I had recorded the morning session. I played back the recording for her and she broke into tears. She pulled a photograph out of her wallet and the image perfectly matched the description of the older man I had described earlier that day. Since then, I limit myself to one group session per day. I have also asked my guides to keep the messages anchored to the client or group that is physically present at the time.

Occasionally, I have received messages that are intended to be delivered by the client rather than to them. I have had clients say to me, "That doesn't sound like anything for me... but, my neighbor/friend just went through..." The guides don't make mistakes. That person was chosen to deliver the message for a reason. Their closeness to the other person, their shared experiences, or, perhaps, an unresolved issue made them the right person for the task.

The point is that we need to come to know and trust our guides. Don't be afraid to ask them to clarify. Sometimes the entities get so excited about actually being able to connect that they go into overdrive. Ask the guides to slow it down. They know us and our limitations but it doesn't hurt to remind them once in a while.

Going Public

In 2013 I had the opportunity to meet and talk with noted psychic, John Edward. It was after one of his large group readings when he gathered together with a small select group, which he refers to as "The Five," for an informal question and answer session. It was reassuring to me that he acknowledged me as a fellow practitioner rather than merely an observer in the audience. Before I said a word, he looked at me and said, "You have a gift," and, "You are pure." I had not yet begun to publicly promote myself as a medium and the recognition was confirming that I was going in the right direction.

I asked him, "When, how, and why did you decide to go public with your abilities?" As I was beginning to "come out," as my wife loves to put it, I was deeply concerned with the public perception of our practice. I was teaching at a public high school. What would the principal or members of the school board say about a psychic in front of a classroom full of impressionable teenagers?

John told me that he had felt exactly the same way. He worked as a technician in a blood lab. Would the boss get mad and fire him? What would his friends say? (Like me, his family pretty much already knew he had "abilities" and considered him a little weird anyway.) All the same fears that I was experiencing had at one time held him back. He decided to take a leap of faith and as a result, his career as a professional psychic took off. We have to, at some point, accept our abilities, and along with them, our responsibilities.

As I confronted my fears, I also began to realize that who I am and what I do is all part of my spiritual path. Not unlike religious faiths, mediumship brings me closer to my understanding of and personal relationship with the force that I perceive as God. Would, or even could, an employer (or in my case, school board) impinge upon my Constitutional right to freely practice my "religion" on my own time, outside of the classroom or workplace? I realized that if I preached Bible lessons from a church pulpit on Sundays, they couldn't fire me for it.

Admittedly, there are times when it gets a little awkward with co-workers when they learn about what I do. Usually, however, it doesn't take long before they are telling me about this or that deceased relative and the strange occurrences they've encountered. Stepping into the public spotlight came with fear and trepidation, but for me to fully accept my gifts, I felt obligated to use them.

Psychic Etiquette

It is vitally important at this point to discuss what I refer to as "psychic etiquette." Have you ever had a complete stranger come up to you and start up a conversation? You know how awkward it is when someone who is not privy to your personal experiences butts into a conversation you're having with close friends.

As a psychic, I can and often do hear, feel, and sense things from complete strangers on the street, in restaurants, or at the grocery store. As much as I want to go up to these people and help them with what I perceive to be their problem or need, it's not like holding the door for someone with an arm load of shopping bags. Connecting with a deceased loved one is a very intimate and personal matter. John Edward refers to these as "ambush readings."

These unsolicited messages can not only frighten people (Who the **** are you and how did you know that my mother died?), they can bring up deep emotional trauma that should not be dealt with in public. One afternoon while sitting a in friend's living room I had a brief but very vivid vision. The friend was the lead singer of a band I played drums with and we had just finished a rehearsal in her basement. We all accepted her mother's invitation to relax and have some snacks up in the living room. As her mother was coming into the room with a tray of drinks I asked her who the old man was. Her mom looked puzzled and asked who I was referring to.

I described an old man with a Santa Claus white beard. He was wearing denim coveralls and work boots, and had a red bandanna sticking out of his left rear pocket. Oh, yes, and he was sitting in the rocking chair on the left side of the room. Her mother smiled awkwardly, there were noticeable tears in her eyes, and her hands shook slightly as she set down the tray of drinks. I had just described Grandpa to the letter.

Although my friend's mom was very polite, I realized at that moment not everyone is eager to embrace what we mediums do.

There are those times when I feel compelled to deliver a message to someone I've just met, even a complete stranger. When that happens I have found a method that works well for me. First, I write my impressions down on a piece of paper, paper bag, napkin, or anything I can find. I hold on to it and don't show it to anyone. Then I strike up a conversation. I might make a comment about the weather, traffic, the food or drink at the restaurant, or just about anything except the message I want to deliver. If the need is truly there to do a reading, I watch and listen for the moment of recognition. That's when I introduce myself and offer my services.

If they are receptive, I can then present the notes I had written down earlier. If they are not comfortable discussing the subject with me right then and there, I give them my business card. (And yes, I do have a "Psychic Medium" business card.) They may not call right away, but that's ok. It could be days, weeks, or even years before I hear from them. Remember, there is no time on the other side. I have made the contact and they will let me know if and when they are ready. They may find another medium or method to bring the message. It might even be part of their life lesson is to move on without the message.

In writing this book, I have recounted many of the experiences I've had over the years. In a lot of the passages I refer to the clients simply as the homeowner or the friend. Sometimes I will use a single initial to keep track of them throughout the retelling. The only times where I use the client's full name is when they have given me written permission to do so. I respect their privacy and it is essential that we all do the same. As a psychic and medium, I am given access to private conversations, events, and emotions that are often very personal. I believe that it is our obligation to hold ourselves to the same standards as counselors and therapists. When doing group or public sessions it is essential that everyone knows that secrets may be revealed in order that anyone who declines may be excused.

Conclusion?

In my practice, I enlist the aid of my spirit guide, Marie, and the rest of the 15 to help earthbound spirits achieve transition and the living achieve the assistance they need along their paths. If we accept that spirits can be earthbound, then it must stand to reason that there is something beyond Earth. Marie, who is not bound by the constraints of space or time, led me to a place that I could easily call heaven. I would not begin to assume that one image or concept of the beyond is the only one and true answer. My experiences have led me to where I am today and it is entirely possible that my explanation of life after death and before birth is for me alone. This is how it has been revealed to me. There is only one way to find out the absolute truth, and I don't think that I'm quite ready for that yet.

Frank Chodl and Betz McKeown, 2012

* * Namaste * *

For more information on the topics covered in this book please check out these books and websites:

Anasazi, History of the, http://pages.swcp.com/~spsvs/outdoors/anasazi/history.html

Association for Research and Enlightenment, A.R.E. Search for Atlantis Findings, www.edgarcayce.org/are/atlantis.aspx,

Astral Projection, How to Perform, www.wikihow.com/Perform-Astral-Projection

Biltmore Estate, Asheville, NC. www.biltmore.com

Bimini Road, www.crystalinks.com/biminiroad.html

Browne, Sylvia, www.sylviabrowne.com/site

Butler, Tom and Lisa, "There is No Death and There are No Dead: Dr. Konstantin Raudive," AA-EVP Publishing, 2003, http://atransc.org/circle/konstantin_raudive.htm

Calvin, John, www.historylearningsite.co.uk/John_Calvin.htm

Cayce, Edgar, www.edgarcayce.org/

Crystal Links, "Astral Projection," www.crystalinks.com/astral.html

Dickenson, Charles M. "The Absent Ones," excerpt from "Poems of Home: V," 1904, www.bartleby.com/360/1/192.html

Dube, Ryan, "List of Psychic Abilities," http://paranormal.lovetoknow.com/List_of_Psychic_Abilities

Edward, John, http://johnedward.net/#

Gulick, Donna, www.DonnaSpringGulick.com

Healing Touch: Healing Beyond Borders, www.healingbeyondborders.org/

Hefner, Alan G. "Xenoglossy", www.themystica.com/mystica/indexes/a.
html, The MYSTICA, February, 2014

Hoppe, Geoffrey, "What is Channeling?" www.crimsoncircle.com/
Library/WhatIsChanneling.aspx

Lightweaver, Michael, Mountain Light Sanctuary, www.mtnlightsanc
tuary.com

Laszlo, Ervin, "Science and the Akashic Field: An Integral Theory of
Everything." www.dankunlimited.com/uno_pound_sharing/Know_
files/-Science-and-the-Akashic-Field-Ervin-Laszlo.pdf

Lilly-Bower, Karen C., Salisbury, NC Ghost Walk, www.salisburyghostwalk.
com/home

Long Island Paranormal Investigators, "Poltergeists and Other Types of
Ghosts: Paranormal Terms and Definitions," 2014, www.ghoststudy.
com/types.html

Manchester Paranormal Investigations, "Types of Paranormal Activity
& Haunts," http://manchesterparanormal.org/Types-of-Paranormal-
Activity.php

McKeown, Betz, www.BetzMcKeown.com

Michie, David, "Do animals have souls that go to heaven? The Buddhist
view", http://davidmichie.com/blog/2015/01/20/do-animals-have-
souls-that-go-to-heaven-the-buddhist-view/, Jan. 2015

Montgomery, Ruth, www.near-death.com/experiences/paranormal04.html

Museum of Talking Boards, History of the Talking Board, 2015, www. museumoftalkingboards.com/history.html

Our Curious World, "Ghosts and the Paranormal: Understanding the Different Types of Ghosts," www.ourcuriousworld.com/Typesof Ghosts.htm

Psychic Abilities & Forms of Prophesy, List of, www.psychic-junkie.com/ list-of-psychic-abilities.html

Second Vatican Council, www.ewtn.com/library/COUNCILS/V2 ALL.HTM

Satan in the Bible, Origin of, www.allaboutgod.com/history-of-satan.htm

Spain, Margo, Wayside Irish Pub, www.waysideirishpub.com/

Tressabelle, "Preparing Divination Tools for Use," February, 2013, https://tressabelle.wordpress.com/2013/02/17/preparing-divination-tools-for-use/

Virtue, Doreen, "Archangels 101: how to connect closely with archangels Michael, Raphael, Gabriel, Uriel, and others for healing, protection, and guidance," 1st ed. 2010. www.hayhouse.com.

Van Praagh, James, http://www.vanpraagh.com/ www. jvpschoolofmysticalarts.com

Warren, Ed and Lorraine, New England Society for Psychic Research in Monroe, Connecticut, www.warrens.net

Zimmerman Jones, Andrew, Quantum Physics Overview, http://physics. about.com/od/quantumphysics/p/quantumphysics.htm

CPSIA information can be obtained
at www.ICGtesting.com
Printed in the USA
LVHW112201240320
651123LV00002B/500